797,885 books
are available to read at

Forgotten Books

www.ForgottenBooks.com

Forgotten Books' App
Available for mobile, tablet & eReader

ISBN 978-1-334-39889-6
PIBN 10766148

This book is a reproduction of an important historical work. Forgotten Books uses state-of-the-art technology to digitally reconstruct the work, preserving the original format whilst repairing imperfections present in the aged copy. In rare cases, an imperfection in the original, such as a blemish or missing page, may be replicated in our edition. We do, however, repair the vast majority of imperfections successfully; any imperfections that remain are intentionally left to preserve the state of such historical works.

Forgotten Books is a registered trademark of FB &c Ltd.
Copyright © 2015 FB &c Ltd.
FB &c Ltd, Dalton House, 60 Windsor Avenue, London, SW19 2RR.
Company number 08720141. Registered in England and Wales.

For support please visit www.forgottenbooks.com

1 MONTH OF FREE READING

at

www.ForgottenBooks.com

By purchasing this book you are eligible for one month membership to ForgottenBooks.com, giving you unlimited access to our entire collection of over 700,000 titles via our web site and mobile apps.

To claim your free month visit:
www.forgottenbooks.com/free766148

* Offer is valid for 45 days from date of purchase. Terms and conditions apply.

English
Français
Deutsche
Italiano
Español
Português

www.forgottenbooks.com

Mythology Photography **Fiction**
Fishing Christianity **Art** Cooking
Essays Buddhism Freemasonry
Medicine **Biology** Music **Ancient Egypt** Evolution Carpentry Physics
Dance Geology **Mathematics** Fitness
Shakespeare **Folklore** Yoga Marketing
Confidence Immortality Biographies
Poetry **Psychology** Witchcraft
Electronics Chemistry History **Law**
Accounting **Philosophy** Anthropology
Alchemy Drama Quantum Mechanics
Atheism Sexual Health **Ancient History**
Entrepreneurship Languages Sport
Paleontology Needlework Islam
Metaphysics Investment Archaeology
Parenting Statistics Criminology
Motivational

OF

CORFE CASTLE,

IN

THE ISLE OF PURBECK.

DORSET.

BY

THOMAS BOND, B.A.

LONDON :
EDWARD STANFORD, 55, CHARING CROSS, S.W.

BOURNEMOUTH :
E. M. & A. SYDENHAM, ROYAL MARINE LIBRARY.

1883.

All Rights Reserved.

CRITICAL NOTICES

Of the above Work.

. . . . . A really excellent book on Corfe Castle. It is one of the best books of the kind I have ever seen. It contains all the information that is extant on the subject, well considered and digested without any rigmarole. The woodcuts are excellent both in drawing and engraving.—*The late J. H. Parker, Esq., C.B.*

From the "Genealogist."

We cordially commend this admirable monograph to the attention of our readers. It is a work of genuine research. From early chronicles, public records, etc., Mr. Bond has been able to construct a most reliable and instructive account of this grand example of mediæval military architecture. The historical portion is eminently readable. The particulars as to the fabric are also well worthy of close study by the serious student of records; and the illustrations are not only well selected but are executed in a very artistic manner.

From the "Archæological Journal."

In the volume before us is embodied an able paper on Corfe Castle, from the pen of Mr. Bond, which appeared in this Journal in 1865, with emendations and improvements, as further researches during the last twenty years have rendered necessary.

Mr. Bond's work treats of the history of Corfe Castle, both architectural and documentary in a most exhaustive way, and it is difficult to see what further can be said about it in its present condition.

From "Notes and Queries."

Corfe is one of the most interesting castles in England. If it cannot compare with Pevensey, which stands beside, and may be said to grow out of the walls of a Roman town, nor with the shell-keep of Berkeley, and the fortified hill of Pontefract in historic interest, Corfe has claims of its own which put it in the very first rank. Corfe alone of all the castles now remaining can show within its enclosure fragments which, without violence to the understanding, may be held to be of an earlier date than the Norman conquest.

We think that Mr. Bond has proved that the site of Corfe Castle was a possession of the Crown when the Domesday survey was made, although that record cannot be quoted in evidence.

Mr. Bond has given a series of extracts from the fabric rolls, which begin in the reign of Henry III. Some of the entries are very interesting.

From the "Antiquarian Magazine."

We have here a book to which we can conscientiously pay a high tribute of praise. The noble ruins of mediæval castles in which England is so pre-eminently rich have rarely found competent historians, for the reason that while, on the one hand, their architecture is a special study, and understood by only a very few, who have made it their own subject; on the other hand those who have thus acquired the necessary general knowledge are too often lacking in the special local knowledge, which is in such cases, absolutely essential. Mr. Bond, however, has unquestionably succeeded in combining these two qualifications. In the present work he gives us, in an enlarged and final form, the results of those valuable researches on the castle, of which the outline has previously appeared in the third edition of Hutchins' "Dorset," and in his paper read before the Archæological Institute, in 1866.

We gladly call attention to the valuable searches made by Mr. Bond among original MS. authorities in the Public Records, especially the instructive "Fabric Rolls." The careful excavations which he has been permitted to make have also led to important results, and, in short, we have in his book the fruits of long and patient study on the spot, combined with an unsparing and yet critical use of all available sources of original information.

We must not omit to notice the excellent plans and illustrations, with which the volume is liberally adorned, and which, by their great clearness are admirably adapted to their purpose.

From the "Athenæum."

Mr. Bond's monograph on Corfe Castle far exceeds in scope its immediate object; it can be read with interest by those who may never set foot in Purbeck. He has illustrated the construction, maintenance, victualling, and furnishing of a mediæval castle, from the time of King John to the Civil War, with a life-like truth that a contemporary account, be it only an inventory or a Fabric Roll, can alone supply.

Nor is the insight afforded by Mr. Bond's excerpts limited to the domain of picturesque antiquarianism. He has supplied many valuable indications regarding the introduction of glass and sea-borne coal into the south of England, the management of the royal forests, the payment and apportionment of labour, and the employment of building materials during the twelfth, thirteenth, and fourteenth centuries.

The engravings that illustrate this book are accurate and interesting, and the photographic facsimiles of the map and bird's-eye view of the castle, drawn by Sir C. Hatton's steward in the year 1588, are far superior in authenticity to the repetitions of those drawings given by Hutchins in his county history.

From the "Bookseller."

The author of this work contributed to the third edition of Hutchins' "History of Dorset" a paper on Corfe Castle. In 1866 he revised the article, and read it before the Archæological Institute at Dorchester. Both of the papers have been re-written for the present volume. In order to make his work accurate, the author has carefully examined the famous fortress, "which is fast crumbling away, or becoming concealed from view by ivy, which is assisting time in the work of destruction." He has also made enquiries in the Public Record Office, the Pipe, the Liberate, the Close, and the Patent Rolls, and discovered other documents, the result being a monograph of particular interest, in which the annals of the Purbeck Island Castle are fully set forth. Mr. Bond imparts additional interest to his volume by adding a ground-plan and a bird's-eye view from photographic facsimiles, of drawings by Ralph Treswell, steward of Sir Christopher Hatton (1588), then owner of the castle.

From "The Reliquary,"

The author of this volume had ample materials for the drawing up of an account of surpassing interest, and he has made use of those materials in a manner most satisfactory, and produced a work that is at the same time masterly, comprehensive and strictly reliable. The volume is altogether one of the most interesting and useful that has yet been devoted to any of our old castles, and we cordially welcome its appearance.

From the "Revue Historique."

"M. T. Bond nous apporte maintenant l'histoire d'un des châteaux le plus importants de l'Angleterre: Corfe Castle. . . . . L'ouvrage est un très exact et favorable spécimen de recherches originales condensées sous un forme concise, sans degressions inutiles, vive et pittoresque."

From "The Times."

Mr. Bond, who has directed much time and trouble to his subject, has done as much as may be towards reconstructing the Castle. He has gathered up its associations with care and conscientiousness, sifting them and rejecting all that are apocryphal, so that his book may be regarded as thoroughly trustworthy. . . . . Even after legend has been brought to the aid of history, enough of indisputable facts remain to make Corfe wonderfully interesting. . . . . Mr. Bond gives incidentally in the course of his interesting narrative many quaint and curious details as to Corfe and manners in the Isle of Purbeck, from the days of the Conqueror and the Norman Kings down to those of the Stuarts and Cromwells."

LOCAL PRESS.

From the "Dorset County Chronicle."

Anyone imbued with the slightest degree of antiquarian taste must peruse Mr. Bond's book, not only with interest but with genuine delight. . . . . . It is a masterly history not merely of local interest but deserves the attention of all archæologists, especially of those who have made the Castle Fortresses of England a matter of investigation. We believe it will henceforth be considered the best authority extant on the ancient stronghold.

"Salisbury and Winchester Journal."

The little work of Mr. Thomas Bond, just issued, will be welcomed as supplying a want which has long existed, of a detailed account of Corfe Castle. . . . . . Mr. Bond's name, we need scarcely say, is well known in connection with antiquarian research in Dorsetshire. . . . . . It is a matter of satisfaction that a building of so much historical interest should have been the subject of such careful and accurate inquiry as Corfe Castle has secured at the hands of Mr. Bond.

"The Sherborne Journal."

The History and Description of Corfe Castle has been again written, and by a competent hand. Both as an antiquary and a Dorset man, Mr. Bond carries an authority with him in this work which can scarcely be said to have attached to previous writers. In the section devoted to a description of the ruins, and to the fabric, Mr. Bond enters at great length into the architectural features of the building, illustrating his ideas with plans and pictures.

"The Bournemouth Visitors' Directory."

Mr. Bond has given us a most valuable contribution to local history, and his work will be read with interest, not only by residents and visitors in this neighbourhood, but by many others interested in antiquarian researches in general history.

"The Bournemouth Observer and Guardian."

Mr. T. Bond, of Tyneham, has produced a work which nationally is of considerable value; which to archæologists is one of especial interest, and which locally will be hailed with much satisfaction—none the less because written by a gentleman whose name is closely identified with the neighbourhood, and because of the thorough earnestness and unflagging enthusiasm with which he directed himself to the task.

"Wareham Advertiser."

. . . . . It is gratifying that Mr. Bond has been spared to publish the work and been enabled to hand down to posterity information which he has been gleaning for the greater part of his life, it being more valuable from the scrupulous accuracy with which he has given the particulars, supported as they are by documents in every instance. The public will, doubtless, be pleased to have placed in their hands such a faithful and interesting account of this ancient fabric.

From the "Wilts Mirror."

The History and Description of Corfe Castle is an admirable work. Mr. Bond has succeeded in an eminent degree in producing a most comprehensive and reliable work, the merits of which will be appreciated, we trust, as their worth, alike by the general reader and those to whom such a work appeals with special interest.

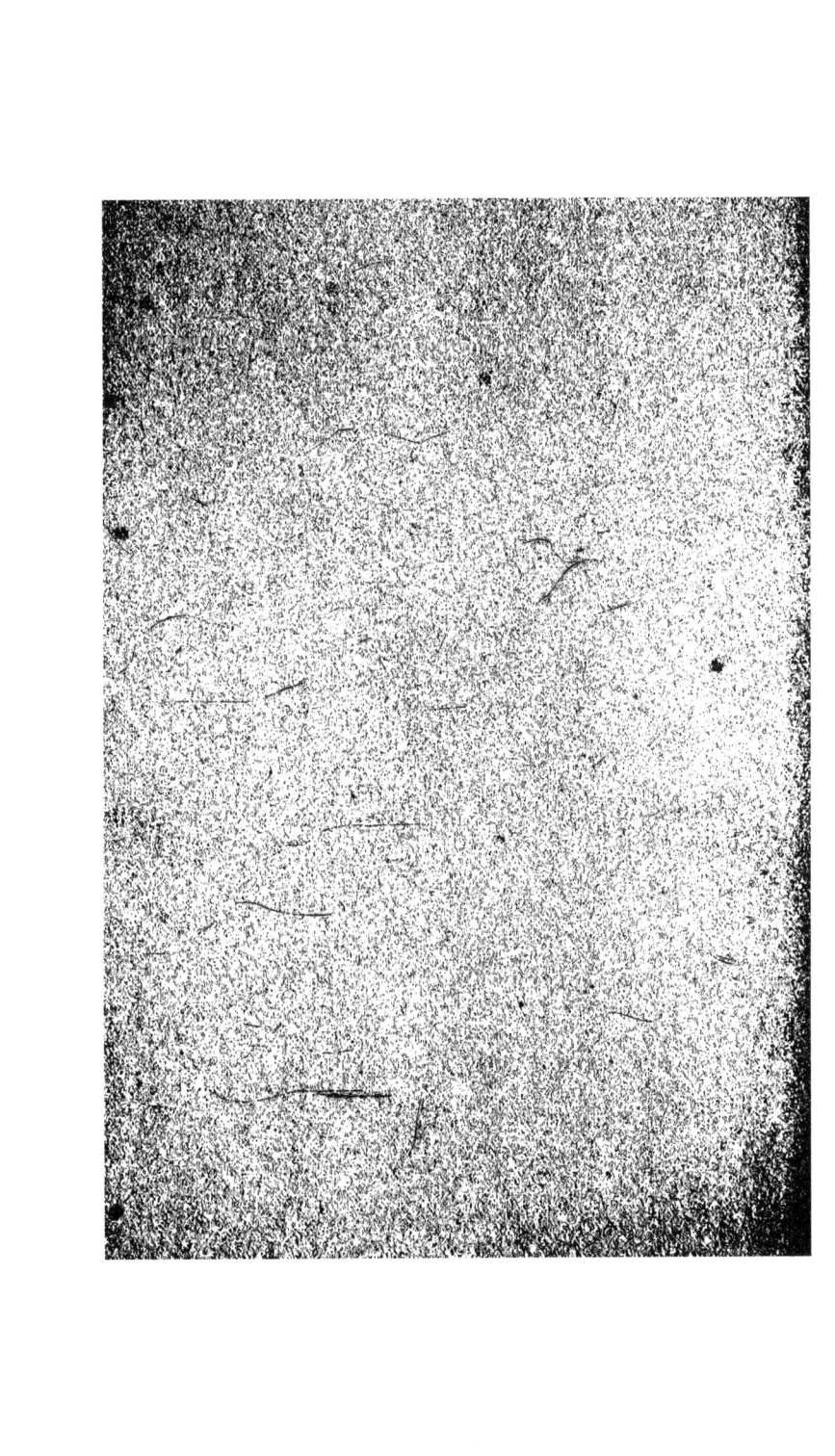

CORFE CASTLE FROM THE WEST.

HISTORY AND DESCRIPTION

OF

CORFE CASTLE,

IN

THE ISLE OF PURBECK,

DORSET.

BY

THOMAS BOND, B.A.

LONDON:
EDWARD STANFORD, 55, CHARING CROSS, S W
BOURNEMOUTH:
E. M. & A. SYDENHAM, ROYAL MARINE LIBRARY.
1883.
All Rights Reserved.

HISTORY AND DESCRIPTION

OF

CORFE CASTLE,

IN

THE ISLE OF PURBECK,

DORSET.

BY

THOMAS BOND, B.A.

LONDON:
EDWARD STANFORD, 55, CHARING CROSS, S.W.
BOURNEMOUTH:
E. M. & A. SYDENHAM, ROYAL MARINE LIBRARY.
1883.
All Rights Reserved.

DA 690
.C73B7

BOSTON PUBLIC LIBRARY

B. H.
May 12, 1894.

PREFACE.

A brief account of Corfe Castle was published in 1773, by Mr. Hutchins, in his "History of Dorset," a work of so much excellence that it has gone through three editions. The author had but little acquaintance with the chronology of architecture, he thought that "King Edgar was probably the founder of this magnificent structure;" and he refers, without disapproval to the supposition of Dr. Thomas Gale, that "Edgar sent for workmen out of Italy for the purpose."

Though in the present day we may be tempted to smile at these conjectures, they may well be excused, for it was not until within comparatively recent times that the architectural features of ancient buildings, whether military, ecclesiastical, or domestic, which help to determine their dates, have seriously engaged the attention of antiquaries. When Hutchins wrote, too, the national archives were almost sealed books, for the cost of examination rendered them practically inaccessible to the public, and he never consulted them. This difficulty has now been removed, and for some years past they have been freely and liberally thrown open to literary enquirers.

Availing myself of these sources of information, I was able to contribute to the third edition of Hutchins' valuable work an amended and much enlarged account of Corfe Castle; and the same was afterwards reproduced in an abridged and somewhat altered form, in a paper, read at a meeting of the Archæological Institute, at Dorchester, in 1866, and printed in the Journal of that Society.

These two accounts have been revised, corrected, and considerably enlarged for the present work. The whole of the subject matter has been rearranged and rewritten, and has been divided into several sections for convenience of reference.

Every part of the ruin has been carefully examined and minutely described, in order that some record might be preserved of many interesting features which are fast crumbling away, or becoming concealed from view by the immoderate growth of ivy, which is assisting time in the work of destruction.

Some diggings which, by the kind permission of the owner, W. R. Bankes, Esq., I have recently made within the castle, have brought to light some curious facts, which afford much food for conjecture; and as it has been thought desirable that the trenches should be again filled in, I have been the more particular in fully describing what is no longer open to view.

Many early chronicles have been consulted, and extensive researches have been made in the Public Record office. The Pipe, the Liberate, the Close, and the Patent Rolls, together with several inquisitions and other documents, have supplied very valuable information. But the most copious and interesting details relating to the construction of the castle have been obtained from a series of ancient Fabric Rolls, amongst the "Ministers' Accounts," in the office of the Queen's Remembrancer of the Exchequer. These range intermittently from 8th Ed. I. to 1st Rich. II., and give accounts of work done from week to week at different periods by artificers and labourers, such as masons, carpenters, smiths, plumbers, &c. They are very voluminous, but I have only found space to notice such entries as seem to be of special interest—particularly those which by giving the names of towers, apartments, and other portions of the castle, are calculated to assist in making out the arrangement of the fortress before it was destroyed. Other items have been mentioned because they show the cost of labour, skilled or otherwise, as well as of materials and the carriage thereof, and from whence they were procured.

The illustrations will not only give the reader a general idea of the present state of the castle, but will help him (if he is so disposed) to study the details and make out, in some measure, the original arrangement. The destruction, however, is so complete that this result is only very partially and imperfectly attainable.

The ground plan and the bird's-eye view at the end of the volume are photographic facsimiles of drawings in a MS. volume at Kingston Lacey, made in 1588, by Ralph Treswell, steward of Sir Christopher Hatton, then owner of the castle. The volume contains a survey of the manors and property in Purbeck which then belonged to Sir Christopher, and it records various privileges enjoyed by the constables and owners of the castle. It had been made some use of by Hutchins, but having been kindly placed in my hands I have extracted from it additional information of considerable interest.

The ground plans at pages 68, 71, 73, are copies on a reduced scale of original drawings, which I was fortunate enough to discover amongst the papers of the late Rt. Hon. George Bankes, at Kingston Lacey, and of which he kindly permitted me to make tracings. They were on loose sheets and unexplained; but the hand-writing on them is that of the 16th century, and it is most probable they are the work of the industrious Treswell. Having compared them and their measurements with the existing ruins, I found, as I expected that those marked A, B, and C, are evidently intended to represent three floors of the Keep. The dimensions, it is true, do not exactly agree with the ruin as it is now seen, but this may be partly owing to the walls being thicker in the lower story than in the upper one, which would give rather less space for the apartments on the ground floor than for those above it. And the discrepancy may be further accounted for by supposing a want of exactness in Elizabethan measurements.

The plan D, at page 83, was found with the others, and no doubt exhibits some other part of the castle, but I have been unable to appropriate it. It seems to represent an apartment in a tower, for it has windows on three sides and is approached by a long flight of steps.

Such are the authorities made use of for the following pages. To write an amusing book on a dry subject is impracticable. "The story of Corfe Castle" has been written,[*]

[*] By the Rt. Hon. G. Bankes. 8vo. 1855.

but it treats more of the political history of the troubled and interesting times in which Sir John Bankes, who then owned the castle, took a prominent part, than it does of the castle itself. Some modern guide books, while reproducing errors of Hutchins, and introducing others, have enlivened their description by picturesque colouring. I make no attempt to compose an entertaining story; I know not the exact spot where the king was murdered; neither am I able to point out apartments appropriated to the use of the priests. I invent no new names; my aim is simply to submit to the reader such *facts* as I have been able to collect from observation, and from records and chronicles. I take the chronicles as I find them; we have no reason to doubt the main facts which they relate respecting the murder of the Martyr King; but after rejecting the miracles with which some of them embellish the story, we have no further evidence on which we can rely to draw a line between history and fable.

In all cases the authorities are referred to so that the critical reader, if he is so disposed, may examine the evidences and judge for himself of the validity of the deductions.

T. BOND.

Tyneham, November, 1883.

CORFE CASTLE.

HISTORY.

Although Corfe Castle stands pre-eminent amongst the Castles of Great Britain as a grand and noble example of mediæval military architecture, its annals present fewer incidents of a striking character, it figures less frequently in the history of the country than might have been expected when we regard its antiquity, its magnitude, the great natural strength of its situation, and the care and skill with which its fortifications have been constructed. Nevertheless, it has at intervals been the scene of events of great historical importance, though during long periods it is chiefly noticed as a state prison. Even in its latter aspect, however, it can hardly fail to command our interest owing to the character and position of many of the prisoners who have been confined within its walls.

If it is true that "happy is the country which has no history," the same cannot truly be said of a great fortress. Happiness may be little known within it even though wars and tumults which have elsewhere raged may not have approached its walls, for ripples from the distant tempest will have seldom failed to reach it in the persons of prisoners of war or captives for political offences. Such, indeed, has often been the case with Corfe; and even in times of political tranquility no sounds of revelry, no jousts and tournaments, no masks, or Royal festivities are recorded to have taken place here. The silence of this gloomy fortress has rarely been disturbed save by the wail of the captive in his dungeon, or the clank of the warder, as he paced his rounds within the battlements. When we look upon the castle in its present state,—the victim of civil commotion, an emblem of the overthrow of feudal tyranny,—however we may lament the destruction of so noble a building, we are almost tempted to palliate the Nemesis which at length reached the scene of so much misery and wickedness.

Both British and Anglo-Roman history are equally silent respecting this place, but a spot so adapted by nature for a stronghold could hardly have failed to be selected for such a purpose from the earliest period. If, however, there were at any time earthworks here indicative of occupation by primæval races, they have long been obliterated to make way for the fortress which replaced them.

Before the close of the seventh century, however, Corfe must have been a place of consideration, for we are told that the Great St. Aldhelm, then Abbot of Malmesbury, and afterwards Bishop of Sherborne, built a church here, which he would not have done unless there had been a Christian population to frequent it. *(See appendix.)*

The next notice of Corfe shows it to have been in the hands of the Anglo-Saxon kings, at which time it formed part of the great manor of Kingston,—the "ton" of the king,—and it afterwards became the property of the Abbey of Shaftesbury, to which it belonged at the time of the Norman invasion.

The incident which has most contributed to the notoriety of Corfe is the murder of King Edward the Martyr, but this is associated with the spot only, and not with the fortress as we now see it, for it need hardly be said that the event took place before the existing castle was erected.

The murder is thus very briefly alluded to in the *Saxon Chronicle* :—

" 978. This year was King Edward slain, at eventide, at Corfe gate, on the 15th day before the Kalends of April and then was buried at Warham without any kind of kingly honours. There has not been mid Angles a worse deed done than this was since they first Britain land sought. Men him murdered, but God him glorified. He was in life an earthly king; he is now after death a heavenly saint. Him would not his earthly kinsmen avenge, but him hath his heavenly Father greatly avenged. The earthly murderers would his memory on earth blot out, but the Holy Avenger hath his memory in the heavens and on earth wide spread. They who would not erewhile to his living body bow down, they now humbly on knees bend to his dead bones."

The story is related more in detail by most of the ancient chroniclers,* but none of them give contemporary evidence. The tragedy is familiar to every reader of English history, nevertheless, it seems proper to reproduce it here when describing the spot on which it occurred.

King Edgar, as is well known, was twice married. By his first wife he had issue, Edward, who at a very early age became his successor and who is known in history as King Edward the Martyr. The second wife of Edgar was Elfrida, daughter of Ordgar, Earl of Devonshire. It is related that the fame of her transcendant beauty having reached the king's ears, he sent one of his Earls, named Athelwold, to visit her father and ascertain privately whether her charms were as great as they had been represented. Athelwold saw her and immediately became enamoured. He made a false report to his sovereign and won her for himself. Rumours, however, that he had been deceived soon reached the king, and he determined to ascertain the truth with his own eyes. Alarmed at the impending danger, Athelwold entreated his wife to adopt some

---

* By William of Malmesbury, Henry of Huntingdon, Simon of Durham, Hovedon Florence of Worcester, Roger de Wendover, John of Peterborough, Knighton, &c.

means of disguising her charms, but Elfrida had now an opportunity of gratifying her ambition. She exerted all her powers to strengthen her natural beauty and she succeeded in exciting the passion of the king. Edgar caused Athelwold to be assassinated in a wood and Elfrida became his Queen. So great was his love for her that he is said to have granted the whole county of Dorset for her dower, a loose expression which must not be literally accepted. But Elfrida had not yet reached the height of her ambition. It was not sufficient for her to have shared the royal throne through the means of assassination, and she scrupled not, after her husband's death, to make use of a similar agency to become the mother, as well as wife of a king.

A favourable opportunity for placing her own son, Ethelred, on the throne was soon thrown in her way. The temptation was too strong to be resisted, the voice of conscience was hushed, and the innocent and unoffending youth became the victim. It is related that the young king went one day to hunt in a wood, near a town called Warham, which, even at that time, was considered a large one. Near this wood, and distant three miles from Wareham, was the house of his step-mother, Elfrida, at a place called Corvesgate, and Edward, toward the close of the day, feeling weary and thirsty, and recollecting that his brother Ethelred, to whom he was fondly attached, was dwelling there with his mother, he determined to go and see him. His companions, who were few in number, led on by the excitement of the sport had become dispersed in different directions, so that the king found himself alone. Nevertheless, he fearlessly proceeded, little suspecting that like a tame lamb he was going to meet his doom. The Queen, being informed that he was approaching, rejoiced that a favourable opportunity had occurred for accomplishing her wicked design. Surrounded by the satellites of her iniquity she cordially saluted him and, simulating great joy at his arrival, invited him to partake of hospitality. He, however, declined to alight, saying he wished to see and speak to his brother. The Queen therefore that commanded a cup might without delay be given him to drink, in order that whilst he was incautiously taking it her design might the more easily be accomplished.

Thereupon, says the chronicler,* one of her attendants more bold and wicked than the rest, imitating the act of Judas, the betrayer of our Lord, gave the king the kiss of peace, in order to disarm suspicion, at the same time expressing for him most loyal devotion. No sooner, however, had Edward raised the cup to his mouth than the assassin fell upon him and stabbed him with a dagger.

The king, finding himself mortally wounded, put spurs to his horse and attempted to return to his companions, but the effort was vain, for he soon fell lifeless to the ground, and his horse taking fright dragged him some distance entangled in his stirrup. Search being afterwards made for him by his attendants, the blood which had poured from the wound gave indication of what had occurred.

When Elfrida heard that the king was dead she ordered his body to be conveyed to a small house hard by, that the deed which had been perpetrated might not be known. Thereupon the accomplices in her crime dragged the sacred body by the heels and cast it in a brutal manner into the house and covered it over with dirty straw.†

The Queen, being in great anguish of mind lest her execrable crime should be discovered, commanded her servants to carry the body as speedily as possible to a secret and marshy place, *(in locis abditis et palustribus)* where it would the least be suspected to have been buried, so that in course of time it might be forgotten. This being done she retired to a manor of her own called Beer, ten miles distant from Corfe.

* Brompton.
† The author of Brompton's Chronicle relates that in the cottage in which the corpse was temporarily concealed, lived a woman who had been blind from her birth and whom the Queen supported by her alms. To this person, while watching the body at night, the glory of the Lord appeared; the house was filled with a brilliant light, and the woman, overwhelmed with terror, received her sight.

Search being afterwards made for the body, the place where it was concealed was discovered * and thereupon some devout people of Wareham, having conveyed the corpse to the church of St. Mary, in that town, buried it in a plain and homely manner on a spot where religious men afterwards built a wooden church, still standing when Brompton's chronicle was written.

The infamous deed of Elfrida soon became known throughout England, and Alfer, a powerful earl in Mercia, and a faithful adherent of the murdered monarch, removed the sacred body from its place of homely sepulture accompanied by a large procession of bishops, abbots, and magnates of the kingdom, and translated it with much pomp to the abbey of Shaftesbury, where it was ceremoniously re-interred. From this the abbey acquired the apellation of the abbey of St. Edward, though originally dedicated to St. Mary.

Some authors, as Huntingdon, Knighton, and Wendover assert that it was the Queen herself who struck the mortal blow. The ancient monkish chroniclers indulge in recounting the various miracles which accompanied and followed these events but as they are unworthy of a place in history we need not reproduce them here. Sufficient to say they were held to indicate the will of Heaven that the murdered king should be enrolled amongst the army of Saints and Martyrs.

On the spot where the body was concealed, the night after the murder, the faithful subjects of the late king afterwards erected a church, which was still standing when the chronicler wrote. This was, no doubt, what in the time of Henry III

---

* The pious chronicler, with monkish credulity, relates that the place where the body was concealed was made known by a pillar of fire which illuminated the spot, and the spring which rose there afterwards poured forth sweet and clear water, by the use of which many sufferers were daily cured of diseases. The tradition seems to have survived to our own day, for the waters of this spring, which is known as St. Edward's fountain and is situated at the foot of the castle hill, continues to be held in estimation for the cure of weak eyes. The situation of the spring, though in some sense marshy, hardly answers to the description of a secret place, as it is close to the present public road and between that and the adjacent stream. The bridge near the spot still goes by the name of St. Edward's bridge.

was spoken of as the chapel of St. Edward, at Corfe,* and was probably on the site of the present parish church, which is dedicated to St. Edward the Martyr.

As for the once beautiful, but now guilty Elfrida, it is related † that she became extremely penitent, and abdicating her regal state she retired to the abbey of Wherwell, in Hampshire, which she had founded, and there, having clothed her body in hair cloth, she for many years slept at night on the ground without a pillow, and mortified her flesh with every kind of penance.

It is not easy to account for the house *(Domus* or *Hospicium)* at Corfe, whatever was its character, being the residence of Queen Elfrida, for there can be little doubt that long before her time, and afterwards, the spot was the property of the Abbey of Shaftesbury.

We meet with few incidents of an important character connected with Corfe Castle during the first six reigns after the Norman conquest, unless (which is not impossible) some of the events which are related to have occurred at Wareham really took place at Corfe.

That the castle had become a fortress of great strength and importance within twenty years after the compilation of Domesday book, is proved from its having been selected by King Henry I. for the incarceration of his unfortunate elder brother, Robert Curthose, Duke of Normandy, who having been vanquished at the battle of Tinchebrai, in 1106, was sent a prisoner to England. According to Benedict, Abbot of Peterborough,‡ Corfe *("Chorf")* was the first place in England where he was confined. How long he remained there is uncertain, but he was ultimately removed to Cardiff, where he died after a wearisome captivity of twenty-eight years.

When the Empress Matilda, assisted by her half-brother, Robert, Earl of Gloucester, had raised the standard of revolt against the usurpation of King Stephen, the war spread into

---

* Liberate Roll. † Malmesbury, Gesta Regum. ‡ Ed. Stubbs, pp. 329—30

every quarter of the kingdom, and of the strongholds of the barons some remained faithful to the king, whilst others passed into the hands of the invader. Amongst the latter were Corfe and Wareham, which in 1137, in the 3rd year of the king's reign, were fortified by the Earl on behalf of his sister.* Corfe afterwards fell again into the king's hands, for in the 15th year of King Stephen it was attacked by Baldwin de Redvers, Earl of Devon, and delivered up to him by the Governor. The king's attempt to retake it was unsuccessful.

In the time of King John, William de Braose, a powerful baron, to whom King Henry II. had given the whole kingdom of Limerick, falling into disgrace, for reasons which are differently related by the chroniclers, fled into France; but his wife, who by some is called Maud de Waleric, and by others, Maud de Haya, and also William, his son, were taken prisoners. According to one authority, they were confined in the Castle of Corfe and died there, but Matthew of Westminster, says that they were "miserably famished at Windesore" by the king's command.†

In 1198, Griffin, Prince of Wales, who had frequently invaded England, having at length been captured, was sent a prisoner to Corfe.‡

Arthur, Duke of Britany, rightful heir to the Crown of England, son of Geoffrey, Duke of Britany, the elder brother of King John, having taken arms against his uncle, the latter besieged him in 1202, in the castle of Mirabeau, in Poictu, and took him prisoner, together with his sister, the Princess Eleanor, and two hundred knights. Arthur is supposed to have been murdered at Rouen by King John; but the Princess, who is sometimes called "the Damsel of Bretagne," and from her personal attractions "the Beauty of Britany," having inherited her brother's legal right to the throne, according to the rule of primogeniture, was brought to England and kept a

---

* Annals of Winton.   † See Dugdale, Baronage, 1. 415 et seq.   ‡ Annals of Winton.

close prisoner for the rest of her life. She is said to have been confined for forty years in Bristol Castle, where she died; but the whole of her long and wearisome captivity was not passed at Bristol, for it was not till after the death of her uncle that she was removed to that place. For some time she was confined in Corfe Castle, where she still remained at her uncle's decease; and although the incarceration of this young and guiltless princess is generally considered one of the many actions of King John for which his memory has been deservedly stigmatised, his son and successor, King Henry III., who continued her captivity, was little less guilty of injustice. Perhaps some extenuation of the conduct of the latter may be found in the fact that the princess exhibited a dauntless and invincible spirit, constantly insisting on her rights to the crown, notwithstanding the nation, during a whole reign, had acquiesced in its being worn by another. Some further extenuation of the king's conduct in this matter may be found in the fact that the law of primogeniture was then by no means firmly established, and twice since the Norman Conquest it had been disregarded on succession to the throne.

Two other princesses shared the captivity of the beautiful and high-spirited Eleanor, during her residence at Corfe, and were her companions there. These were Margery and Isabel, the two daughters of William, King of Scotland, who, notwithstanding he had sworn fealty to King John, had engaged to marry one of his daughters to the Earl of Boulogne, without the sanction of the King of England. This, by the feudal law, was a serious infringement of the rights of the overlord, and King John summoned the King of Scots to answer for his presumption, and also marched a powerful army into Scotland to enforce the demand. King William, in order to appease a powerful neighbour, delivered his daughters into the hands of the King of England, at whose pleasure they were to be disposed of in marriage. How long they remained at Corfe is uncertain, but in the following reign they were married, the one to Hubert de Burgh, the Justiciary, the other to the Earl Marshall.*

The cruelties of King John were so intolerable that numbers of men and women, both rich and poor fled to foreign parts, and even the Queen herself was at one time placed in strict confinement *(sub arcta custodia)* in Corfe Castle.† It has been thought by some that, in revenge for her husband's infidelity, she had pursued a similar course, but this is considered by Dr. Lingard and Sir Thomas Hardy to be questionable. It is certain, however, that she was closely watched and strictly guarded.

Some curious and interesting details, have come down to us ‡ respecting articles supplied for the use of the royal ladies, while they remained at Corfe, which show that they enjoyed many indulgences, and were maintained in a style becoming their rank.

29th June, 15th John, 1213, the mayor and reeves of Winchester were commanded to supply to the Queen, the king's niece, and the two daughters of the King of Scotland, who were at Corfe, such robes and caps and all other things necessary for their vestment as Robert de Vipont should demand; the cost to be repaid at the king's exchequer.

6th July, 15th John, the mayor of Winchester was commanded to send in haste to the king, for the use of his niece Eleanor, and the two daughters of the king of Scotland, robes of dark green, namely, tunics and supertunics, with capes of cambric, and fur of miniver, and twenty-three yards of good linen cloth; also, for the use of the king's niece, one good cap of dark brown, furred with miniver, and one hood for rainy weather, for the use of the same; besides robes of bright green for the use of their three waiting-maids, also tunics and supertunics and cloaks with capes of miniver, or rabbit skins, and furs of lamb skins, and thin shoes for the use of the daughters of the King of Scotland,

* Lingard   † Gervase of Canterbury II. 102.   ‡ In the Close Rolls.

the king's niece, and her three waiting-maids. Also for the use of the king's niece one saddle with gilded reins; and the mayor is to come himself with all the above articles to Corfe, there to receive the money for the cost of the same.

6th Aug. 15th John, the mayor and reeves of Winchester were ordered to send, without delay, to Corfe constabulary for the use of the king's niece, a beautiful saddle with scarlet ornaments and gilded reins.

15th July, 16th John, Peter de Mauley was commanded to procure for the king's niece, who is in the custody of Robert de Vipont, one scarlet robe, namely a cloak and a tunic with cendal, and another for the wife of Robert de Vipont; and also for the king's niece some good and fine linen cloth, enough to make four or five chemises and four sheets; not, however, of the king's finest cloth, but rather if they have none suited for this except the king's finest cloth, to purchase it as good as they can with the king's money; and she is also to have two pair of boots delivered to her by the messenger of Robert de Vipont, the bearer of this order.

The mayor and reeves of Winchester were commanded to cause to be supplied without delay to Robert de Vipont and William de Harcurt, for the use of the king's niece, a cap for rainy weather, a riding saddle, shoes, and sixty yards of linen cloth. Also shoes for the use of the daughters of the King of Scotland; and the cost to be accounted to them at the exchequer.

In 5th Henry III. the barons of the exchequer were ordered to make allowance to Peter de Mauley of 7,000 marks, demanded of him as part of his fine made with King John, for having married the daughter and heir of Robert de Turnham, which he laid out on the works of Corfe Castle, and in the expenses consequent upon the custody of Eleanor the king's cousin, the custody of the daughters of the King of Scotland, and the custody of Richard, the king's brother; and also in the expenses incurred by King John at divers times at Corfe, after Lewis, the French king's son had landed in England.

6th Henry III. the treasurer and chamberlains of the exchequer were ordered to pay to Andrew Buckerel £6 14s. 2d., which he laid out, by the king's command, in the following articles—namely: a silken couch, price £1 10s. 1d., and delivered to John de Cundi, for the use of Eleanor, the king's cousin, and Isabella, daughter of the King of Scotland; two coverlets of fine linen, price £2 2s. 1d., likewise for their use; and six yards and a-half of scarlet, price £1 3s., to make two coverlets, also for the use of the same; and six yards and a-half of dark green, price 13s., to make a robe for the use of their waiting maid; one fur of lamb-skin, price 4s., for the use of the same waiting maid; and forty yards of linen cloth, price 21s., for the use of Eleanor and Isabella.

The health of the princess, no less than her clothing, seems to have been an object of the king's solicitude, for in 6th Henry III. Master John de Beauchamp was sent all the way from London to administer medicine to her at Corfe when sick. His journey was probably a hurried one, and the distance being long, the palfrey on which the doctor rode seems to have been overworked, for it died on its way back to London. The treasurer and chamberlains of the exchequer were ordered to pay to its master out of the king's treasury three marks (£2) in compensation.

The prices paid by the mayor and reeves of Winchester, and which the king commanded should be accounted to them by the barons of the exchequer for articles delivered to Robert de Vipont and William de Harcourt for the use of the princeses and their waiting maids, give us an insight into the value of money at that period. £7 17s. was paid for thirty yards of green cloth at the price of 2s. 8d., and for three yards of green cloth at 2s. 4d; a like sum was paid for capes and furs for the use of the same; also 18d. for thin shoes for the two waiting maids.*

* Close Roll.

About the 6th Henry III. the Damsel of Bretagne was removed from Corfe to Gloucester, where she was staying on 7th August in that year, and she was still there on the 23rd July, 7th Henry III. Ten shillings a day were allowed to the Sheriff for her sustenance. After this she was taken to Marlborough, where we find her on the 20th August in that year; but before 12th March, 9th Henry III., she had reached her final destination at Bristol, where she is said to have passed the rest of her wearisome existence. During her residence at Corfe she had no doubt been supplied with venison from the chase of Purbeck, and it continued to be sent to her after her removal. On 9th Feb., 10th Henry III., Hugh de Neville and Roger de Clifford were ordered to send two bucks from the chase of Corfe to Ralph de Williton, for the use of Eleanor, the king's cousin.* Ralph de Williton was her gaoler at Bristol.

The two hundred knights captured at the siege of Mirabeau were sent to different places in England and Normandy, loaded with irons; and on the 4th Feb., 1203, the king issued his commands to the constables of the several castles in which they were at first confined to send twenty-four of them immediately to Corfe Castle, where, according to the Margam annals, twenty-two of them, —the most noble and valorous in arms, were starved to death. That King John had some sinister design which he wished to keep secret with regard to the disposal of these prisoners when he sent them to the remote and secluded fortress of Corfe, may, perhaps, be inferred from the fact that he at the same time addressed a close letter to the constable of the Castle, commanding him to do with them whatever he should be told on the king's behalf, by Thomas, the clerk of the Chambers, and Hugh de Nevill, whom he sent to communicate verbally his instructions. Of these unfortunate victims of loyalty to their legitimate sovereign, the following are some of their names:—Emeric de Luens, Hugh de Oire, Theobald de Veigny, William de Rupe, Gilbert de

* Close Roll.

Chastuner, William de Rad', William de Alers, Long' de Bellomonte, Peter le Petit, Philip de Columbes, Arkenbeld de Columbes, Reginald de Tirepeie, William de Rigaut, Warin Crum, Maurice Basvent, Samuel de Enla, William Brichard, Ernald de Maleschaus, Peter de Sancta Maura, Geoffrey de Waleufre, Philip de la Ferer, Roger Vilain, Chalon de Ponte, and Fulk Gastenell.*

Persons, however, of greater distinction than most of the above, were sent to different places in England and Normandy, loaded with irons, the most prominent of whom were Hugh de Lusignan, Count de la Marche; Geoffrey de Lusignan, brother of Guy, King of Jerusalem; Andrew de Chevenay, William de Rochefocauld, Viscount de Châtelerault, Raimond de Thouars, Savary de Mauleon, Hugh Beauchain, and Peter de Rusiaco.† Whether any of these were confined in Corfe Castle we have no evidence to show, except as regards Savary de Mauleon. He seems to have been sent a prisoner to Corfe, where, probably conspiring with the other captives, he seized the tower of the Castle, and for a time held it against the king. His resistance, however, was not of long duration, for 20th Aug., 5th John, 1203, William de Blundevill, the constable, was commanded to take him safely under a strong escort to the king in Normandy, together with Americ de Forc, and sufficent force is to be left in the Castle to secure its being better guarded in future.‡

If the story told in the Margam annals is true, the murder of the Poictevan victims was probably not long delayed, for 3rd

* Patent Roll, 4th John, m. 3.
† Hardy's description of the Patent Rolls.
‡ Patent Roll, 5th John, m. 7. Savary de Mauleon was soon afterwards released, and he subsequently rose high in the favour of King John, who made him Seneschal of Poictu. In 15th John a safe conduct was given for him and his retinue to come to England, and the Castle of Winchester and the towns of Wareham and Cranborne were committed to his charge. He also became sheriff of the county of Hants, and constable of Porchester Castle. In 17th John he had licence from the king for himself and his heirs to coin money of a limited value, to be current throughout the whole duchy of Aquetain; and in 18th John a general command was issued to the constables, castellans, and keepers of the king's castles, to receive him and his retinue, whether great or small, and to treat him with marked distinction. (*Patent Roll.*)

Oct., 6th John, 1204, the only persons mentioned as having been delivered over by Willian de Blundevill on relinquishing his office of constable to Geoffry de Nevill, his successor, were Gwyomer Briton and Geoffry le Tongre, Knts. Gilbert de Stanford and Alan Goldsmith *(Aurifaber)* of London, together with Alexander, a hostage of J. de C^{r}cy.*

Amongst the many acts of cruelty attributed to King John, the following also is connected with Corfe Castle. It is related by some chroniclers that a certain Peter de Wakefield a layman, living near Pomfret, and thence known as Peter de Pomfret, was so highly esteemed by the common people, that they designated him " Peter the wise man of England.' Having predicted many events which afterwards chanced to come to pass he was regarded as a prophet. Amongst other predictions he foretold that the king would not reign more than fourteen years. The prophecy was in effect fulfilled, but not in a way which was expected; for in the 14th year of his reign John submitted himself and his kingdom to the suzerainty of the Apostolic See. On the day preceding this event, Peter being interrogated by the king, before his whole court, as to how long his reign would continue, intrepidly replied, until the third hour of the following day and no longer. Thereupon, King John being transported with rage, ordered the bold but imprudent prophet to be taken into custody and strictly confined in the Castle of Corfe. He was afterwards, by the king's command, dragged by horses about the town of Corfe, together with his sons, and then hanged.†

In 15th John the king was anxious to put Corfe Castle into a good state of defence, and the Sheriff of Gloucester was directed to send thither, under safe custody, and by a secure route, one Mangonel and one Petrary. Ten thousand quarrels made at Knaresborough were sent to Poole, no doubt to be forwarded to Corfe or Wareham. Some of the king's wine was also sent to Corfe at the same time.‡

---

* Patent Roll, 6th John, m. 8.
† Chronicle of Thomas Wykes—Annals of Waverly.   ‡ Close Roll.

15th Dec., in the same year, Henry de Esturmy was commanded to cause to come to Corfe without delay all the carts which he could procure in his bailiwick, to carry the king's treasure to Portsmouth.*

The King, by letters patent dated at Corfe, 28th Ap., A.R. 16, acknowledges to have received at the hands of William de Harecurt, at Corfe, on Monday, the morrow of the close of Easter preceding, Thomas de Colvill and Gervase Avenel, hostages of the King of Scotland, together with certain other prisoners and hostages of no note therein named.†

6th July, 17th John, the King acknowledged to have received from Thomas de Samford at Devizes, on Monday, the octave of St. Peter and St. Paul, thirty-six bags of money, which came from the treasury at Corfe, and were in keeping of the said Thomas. The bags ought to contain 9,090 marks, and were sealed with the seal of the Bishop of Winchester.‡

1215-16. The king having repudiated the great Charter, with the sanction and concurrence of the Pope, who had released him from his oath to observe it, and had excommunicated the barons who had exacted it, renewed his resistance to his rebellious nobles, and having obtained the aid of foreign forces from the Duke of Brabant, he captured the Castle of Rochester in which were William de Albeni, the governor, Odonel, his son, William de Lancaster, William de Ernesford, Thomas de Muleton, Osbert Gifford, and William D'Abrincis, who were delivered over to Peter de Mauley, and by him sent close prisoners to Corfe Castle, of which he was the constable. The barons, on the other hand, transferred their allegiance to Prince Louis of France, afterwards King Louis VIII., who, by their invitation, had landed in England, and placed himself at their head. He took Winchester, and reduced nearly all the south of England, except Dover and Windsor; but the king reinforced the Castles of Corfe and Wareham,

* Close Roll.
† Patent Roll, 16th John, m. 3. Rymers Fœd. 1, 184.
‡ Patent Roll, 18th John, m. 18.

together with those of Wallingford and Devises, by a large addition of provisions and arms.* The Winton Annals say that the castles were delivered up to him "*usque ad Corwh*,' which looks as if Corfe, notwithstanding the king's precautions, had fallen into the hands of the rebels.

Whilst Corfe Castle is chiefly known in history as a State prison, it is a relief to find that on one occasion at least it was devoted to hospitality. William Longespée, Earl of Salisbury, having been taken prisoner by the King of France at the battle of Bovines, a negotiation was entered into by King John for his liberation, in exchange for Robert, son of Robert, Count de Dreux, then in the king's custody, and soon after this the count himself was expected in England. On 15th May, A.R. 17, 1216, the king wrote to Peter de Mauley, at that time constable of Corfe, commanding him, that if the Count de Dreux should land within his jurisdiction, he should receive him graciously, and should honourably entertain him with hospitality "in our hall in the ward of the Casdle"—("*in aula nostra in ballivo castri*"), and if it should please him to enter the tower (*in turrim entrare*), he is to be permitted to have access thereto and elsewhere.†

18th John. In the summer of this year the king was marching rapidly into the West of England, with the intention of putting Corfe, Wareham, Bere, Sherborne, 'Wells, and Bristol into a position of defence; but in the October following death put an end to his tyrannical reign. During the last 12 years of his life he frequently visited Corfe Castle, but his stay was often limited to a single day, and seldom extended beyond four or five, excepting in the last year, when he remained here from the 23rd June to the 17th July. His last visit was on the 25th August, and was limited to that and the following day.‡

* Matthew Paris.   † Patent Roll, 17th John, m. 1.
‡ Hardy's Itinerary of King John in introduction to the Close Rolls.

4th Henry III., 7th May, Peter de Mauley was peremptorily commanded to come to London for the king's coronation, and to be there on the vigil of Pentecost next, bringing with him the king's brother, and the regalia then in his custody at Corfe.*

In the lawless times which succeeded the death of the Earl of Pembroke, the Protector, during the minority of King Henry III., many of the great barons usurped the king's castles and other possessions of the crown, which they refused to surrender to legitimate authority. Amongst these refractory nobles was conspicuous Peter de Mauley, who held the Castle of Sherborne, with the custody of the shires and forests of Somerset and Dorset†; but in 1221 he was taken prisoner on suspicion of treason, and was liberated on surrendering Corfe.‡

In 5th Henry III. he delivered up the castle to the king, with Eleanor the king's kinswoman, and Isabel, sister of the King of Scots, with all the jewels, military engines, and ammunition therein, which King John had formerly committed to his trust.§

8th August in the same year, the treasurer and chamberlains of the exchequer were ordered to pay to Hubert de Burgh, the justiciary, three hundred marks for the king's use, and for purchasing victuals and other necessaries for provisioning the Castle of Corfe.‖ Soon afterwards they were commanded to pay to Saher de Aldham eighty marks, to be taken to Ralph Gernun and John Russel at Corfe, for the same purpose. ‖

Corfe Castle was one of the strong places which Simon de Montfort Earl of Leicester, and the other rebellious barons required to be delivered up to them by King Henry III.¶ After the death of this earl in the battle of Evesham in 1265,

---

* Close Roll, 4th H. III.   † Trevet annals.   ‡ Annals of Winton
§ Dugdale's Baronage, 1. 734.   ‖ Close Roll. 5, H. III.
¶ Hutchins says it was the third on the list, but the Burton annals place it the twelfth.

his widow fled into France and resided in a convent at Montargis; but his daughter Eleanor having been betrothed to Llewellyn, Prince of Wales, was sent back to her mother in charge of Almeric, her brother. The vessel which bore them was captured near the Scilly Islands, and they were brought to the king, who thereupon placed Eleanor in an honourable position with the queen, but sent Almeric a prisoner to Corfe.*

47th Henry III. Henry, son of Richard, Duke of Cornwall, King of the Romans, on leaving the barons' party received 100 marks out of the issues of the county, from the sheriff, to fortify this castle and that of Sherborne.†

We hear little of Corfe during the reign of King Edward I., except as regards its architecture, respecting which some notice is given in subsequent pages under the head of "The Fabric." The castle was greatly strengthened by new fortifications during this reign.

34th Edward I. Walter de Morreve, or Murray, one of Robert Bruce's followers, was placed in charge of Robert Fitzpain, who was commanded to conduct or send him to the Castle of Corfe, to be securely detained in some safe part of the said castle, where he was to be provided with suitable sustenance.‡

15th Edward II. The king, by writ to John Latimer, orders him to furnish this castle with victuals, &c., out of the issues of his bailiwick under great penalties, and to certify to the treasurer and barons of the exchequer what he may have laid out.§

17th Edward II. After the escape of Roger Mortimer, Earl of March, from the Tower of London, a writ was addressed, amongst many others, to the constable of Corfe Castle, directing him to keep the prisoners in his castle in safe and sure custody, so that he may be able to answer for them at the king's command.‖

* Dugdale's Baronage, 1., 759. † Close Roll, m. 15, Dug. Bar. 1, 765.
‡ Rymer vol. 1, p 1013, 34th Ed. I. § Parl. Writs.
‖ Madox Hist. Excheq., c. X. p. 263.

In 1325 Sir Robert de Walkefare, Knt., a man of crafty and turbulent disposition, "always more ready to stir up commotion than to appease it," was taken prisoner and confined in the Castle of Corfe; but he rose against the constable, whom he murdered, and then escaped to the Continent, where he joined the Queen and Prince Edward, who had been proclaimed public enemies.*

King Edward II. having been captured in Wales by the rebellious barons, 14th Nov., 1326, was in the January following confined at Kenilworth in the custody of the Earl of Leicester, but the Earl treated his royal prisoner with more gentleness and humanity than suited the purpose of the Queen and her paramour. The King was therefore delivered to Lord Berkeley, Sir John Matravers, and Sir John Gournay, who each had charge of him for a month at a time. Lord Berkeley is said to have behaved kindly to him, but the treatment he received from Matravers was the reverse. It was, perhaps, while he was in the power of the latter, who was a Dorsetshire knight, and had a considerable estate in Purbeck, that the unfortunate prince was sent a prisoner to Corfe Castle. But it is not probable that he remained long here: for the sympathy of the people having been awakened by his misfortunes, he was hurried by night, by unfrequented roads, from one fortress to another, in order to conceal his place of residence, till at length he was murdered at Berkeley under circumstances of unspeakable barbarity, 21st Sept., 1327. There can be little doubt, however, that Corfe Castle was the scene of some of the cruelties which were inflicted on him with a view to deprive him of his reason or his life.

The leading part which the Earl of March had taken in the government of the country roused the jealousy of the English nobility; and Edmund Earl of Kent, half brother of the king, who at first took part with Queen Isabella in opposition to his sovereign, soon became dissatisfied with the conduct of public affairs, and disgusted with the abandoned

---

* Walsingham Hist. Angl.

conduct of the queen, as well as with the insolence of her paramour. His change of mind becoming known to Isabella and the Earl of March, they regarded him as a rival, and dreaded the influence he might exercise over the young king, his nephew. They therefore resolved on his destruction, and to this end contrived an extraordinary plot.

The secrecy which was observed in regard to the places in which the late king had been confined made the public hesitate to believe that he was actually dead. The Earl of March availed hinself of their incredulity as a means by which he might compass the destruction of his rival. The Earl of Kent was told by Sir John Matravers that King Edward II. was still alive, and kept in close confinement in Corfe Castle, where none but his domestics were permitted to see him. In order to give semblance to this report, shows and masking were got up, with dancing, upon the towers and walls of the castle, which being perceived by the people of the country, it was thought there was some great king residing in the fortress for whom these entertainments were provided.* On receiving this intelligence the earl proceeded to the neighbourhood of Corfe, in order to ascertain how far the report was true, and finding the surrounding inhabitants believed it, he sent a certain friar to make further inquiries. Semblance of difficulties was thrown in the friar's way, and it was not without great caution that he was admitted into the castle. At length, having corrupted the porter, he gained admission, and lay all day concealed in the porter's lodge. When night came, being disguised as a layman, he was brought into the great hall, where he was shown a person who was sitting royally at supper and, with great majesty, counterfeited the king. The friar was only permitted to get a distant view of the scene, which by such dim artificial light as was at that time in use, was not very distinct. Whether he was really deceived, or was acting as an accomplice, he reported to the earl that he had actually seen the king alive and well, whereupon the latter

* Stow's Chronicle, 129.

affirmed with an oath that he would endeavour by all the means he could to deliver his brother from prison.* Being thus assured of the truth of the report, and having been encouraged by the Pope to endeavour to obtain Edward's release and restoration, the earl asked leave to see his brother. Sir John Deverel, the constable, however, not denying that the king was in the castle, declined to permit an interview, but offered to carry to him any written communication. The Earl of Kent fell into the snare, and a letter which he addressed to Edward was immediately forwarded to Sir John Matravers, and by him shown to the queen and the young king. Thereupon, the earl was arraigned in the Parliament assembled in Winchester in March, 4th Ed. III., when his own letter was produced. In his defence he pleaded that a certain friar preacher in London had conjured up a spirit who assured him that Edward his brother was yet alive, and added that he had been encouraged in his endeavour to restore his brother to liberty by the Lord Zouch, Sir Ingram Berenger, Sir Robert Taunton, Sir Fulk Fitzwarine, Henry Lord Beaumont, and Sir Thomas Rosslyn. Moreover, the Archbishop of York had promised to support him with 5,000 men.† He was, however, condemned of high treason, and was beheaded at Winchester 9th March, 1329. It is said that so strong was the public feeling against the injustice of the sentence, that no one but a condemned criminal could be found to carry it into effect.

King Edward III. occasionally visited the castle. In the 12th year of his reign, disquieting news having reached him, he commanded the constable of Corfe Castle to cause it to be strictly guarded, and to be especially careful that it is not for want of precaution taken either by surprise or attack.‡

20th Ap., 8th Richard II., 1385, the king having heard that his enemies of France and elsewhere were preparing an invasion of England, commanded the mayor, bailliffs and commonalty of his Castle of Corfe and all and singular the

---

* Stow.   † Walsingham.   ‡ Close Roll m. 27, d.

residents of the Isle of Purbeck to give aid to Philip Walwayn, the constable of the castle, in defence of the Is¹e.*

The garrison maintained there in time of peace was a slender one. In 15th Edward II., 1322, Sir John le Latimer, the constable, rendered an account of its cost and also of the outlay for repairs done in the castle in that year. The payments made to the men were as follows: sixteen balistarii or crossbow men, had 4d., ten bowmen *(sagittarii)* 2d., and four men-at-arms 12d. per diem, each. Besides these, every tything of Purbeck being bound to furnish one efficient man at the king's cost, for ten days, in time of disturbance, for defence of the castle; thirty-four such men, of whom six were balistarii and eight foot lancers, received pay at the same rate as the above. Twelve men of the town of Corfe had ½d. a night for keeping watch and ward for forty nights, according to ancient custom.†

The chase or warren of Purbeck and the custody of the castle were often, though not always, entrusted to the same person, and both were occasionally in the hands of the sheriff of the county, as minister of the crown.

40th Henry III. The king committed the *corpus* of the Castle of Corfe to Elias de Rabayne during pleasure, saving to the king the warren, forest, and all other things appurtenant to the castle outside the walls thereof, which latter, so excepted, he committed to the custody of Stephen de Ashton, the sheriff of the county, also during pleasure. At length the custody of the castle and the office of constable were given for more definite periods of time, and 5th Edward III. the custody of the Castle of Corfe and the Warren of Purbeck were granted to Bernard Brocas for his life, and he was to receive for the same the accustomed wages. 14th Richard II., the king granted the office of constable of the Castle of Corfe, with the fees and profits belonging to the same, to his brother Thomas, Earl

* Patent Roll 8th Ric. II., 2 ps. m. 18.
† Miscellanea in the Exchequer, Corfe Castle.

of Kent, and Alice his wife, for their lives. The Earl died 20th Richard II., and afterwards it was given to John Beaufort, Earl of Somerset, in fee. In this family it continued till the attainder of Henry Beaufort, Duke of Somerset, 1st Ed. IV., when it escheated to the crown. In the following year King Edward IV. granted the office of constable to his brother, Richard, Duke of Gloucester, afterwards King Richard III., in tail. He also granted the manor of Corfe, in tail, to George, Duke of Clarence, on whose attainder it once more escheated to the crown. King Henry VII. visited Corfe in the 11th year of his reign, 1496, and remained there from 27th July till 5th August, when he proceeded to Salisbury. He granted the castle and manor to his mother Margaret, Countess of Richmond, for her life. She died 1st Henry VIII. 27th Henry VIII. they were given, together with the Isle of Purbeck, to Henry, Duke of Richmond and Somerset, the king's natural son, on whose death, 28th Henry VIII., they again reverted to the crown.

King Edward VI., A.R. 1 and 2, gave the castle and manor to his uncle, Edward Seymour, Duke of Somerset, and on the duke's attainder they were once more forfeited. Queen Elizabeth, in the 14th year of her reign, granted, or rather sold, for £4761 18s. 7½d., this castle, with its lordship, demesne lands, liberties, and privileges, to Christopher Hatton, Esq., then one of her gentlemen pensioners, who afterwards became conspicuous as Sir Christopher Hatton, the Lord Chancellor. He died 34th Elizabeth, largely indebted to the crown; but dying unmarried, Sir William Hatton, *alias* Newport, son of Sir John Newport, by Dorothy, sister of Sir C. Hatton, was his heir.

Sir William Hatton, *alias* Newport, gave the Castle and most of his lands to his wife, the Lady Elizabeth Cecil, daughter of Thomas, Earl of Exeter, afterwards the second wife of Lord Chief Justice Coke, who sold it in 1635 to Sir John Bankes, Lord Chief Justice, ancestor of W. R. Bankes, Esq., of Kingston Lacay, Dorset, the present owner.

CUSTODES, GOVERNORS, OR CONSTABLES.*

In the reign of Henry III. this castle, and that of Sherborne, were often committed to the sheriff of the counties of Dorset and Somerset.

5, 6 John, William de Blundevil.
    6 —— Galfrid de Nevil, to whom it was delivered Oct. 3. The King directed a writ to the sheriff to cause him to have 50 solidates in lands in Knol, Stuple, and Chrech, which were Robert de Tebovill's, for the custody of the Castle.
    9 —— John de Bassingburn. 8 July, Galfrid de Nevill and his bailiffs of the Castle of Corfe are ordered to deliver the said castle, without delay, to John de Bassingburn.
  17 —— Peter de Mauley, or de Malo Lacu.
... H. III. Luke de Cary, *anno incerto.*
    4 —— Peter de Mauley.
    5 —— John Russel.
    8 —— the Bishop of Bath. Mandatum est Johanni Russel de Sireburn, 12 Dec.
    8 —— Radulph Gernum. 6 Nov. 9 Hen. III. the King orders the treasurer and chamberlains of the Exchequer to pay to Radulph Gernum 30 marks, due to him for the eighth year of his reign, out of the 100 marks per annum which he owed him for the custody of the Castle of Corfe.
  14 —— Peter de Mauley.
  22 —— Richard de Langeford, sheriff, 18 Dec.
  25 —— Hugh de Vivon, 14 Feb.
  33 —— Peter Genevil.
  33 —— being late in the custody of H. Vivon, Will. de Fortibus had orders to deliver it to Barth. Peche.
35 }
36 } —— Elias Rabayne, sheriff.
  37 —— Bartholomew Peche, sheriff.
  39 —— Elias Rabayne, sheriff.
  42 —— Stephen Longespe. Elias Rabayne was ordered to deliver up the castle to him June 22. He is mentioned in the list of Henry the Third's Castles.

---

* From Hutchin's History of Dorset, and the authorities there referred to, with additions.

45 —— Philip Basset: the mandate addressed to Philip de Cerne, sheriff.
45 —— Philip Basset: the mandate addressed to Matthew de Mara, 3 May.
45 —— Matthew de Mara: the mandate addressed to Emmelina, Countess of Ulster, once widow of Stephen Longespe, and the rest of the executors of the said Stephen, who before had the custody of it, 4 Feb.
46 —— Philip Basset, sheriff.
47 —— Nicholas de Moeles of Cadbury: the mandate addressed to Philip Basset, 15 June.
47 —— Peter de Montforte: the mandate addressed to Nicholas de Molis, 16 June.
... —— Nicholas de Molis: the mandate addressed to Philip Basset, 15 Jan.
48 —— Henry Plantagenet, son of Richard, King of the Romans, 15 July.
53 —— Roger Mortimer: the mandate addressed to Alan de Plugenet.
54 —— Alan de Plugenet.
56 —— E. de Rabayne, 24 April.
3, 4 Ed. I. E. de Rabayne.
7 —— Richard de Bosco, as E. Rabayne had it, 29 June.
8 —— John de Cormailes, sheriff.
... —— Richard de Bosco: the mandate addressed to J. Cormailes, 4 March.
10 —— the King committed the castle to Richard de Bosco during pleasure, and to answer at the Exchequer for the issues, as E. de Rabayne had used; also for the issues of the warren of Corfe, and the land which Robert de Mucegros held there, which R. de Bosco bought, for the King's use, for 21 marks, out of 24 marks, which the King's men at Bridport used to pay at the Exchequer, for that vill, for the sustenance of the said Richard, for the custody of the castle, as long as he had it, and to answer yearly at the Exchequer for the residue of the 24 marks during the said term.
... Edw. I. William Monteacute, *anno incerto*.
27 —— Simon Monteacute, 16 Sept.
29 —— Henry de Laci, Earl of Lincoln: the mandate addressed to Simon Monteacute, 29 Jan.
33 —— Robert Fitzpain, 20 March.
34 —— William Monteacute
8 Edw. II. Philip Walwayne, 14 April.

9 Edw. II. Richard Lovel and Muriel his wife, 1, Sept.
11 —— ditto, 25 Oct. the mandate addressed to Roger Damory: with the forest of Purbeck, 20 Feb. the mandate addressed to Richard Lovel.
14 —— John de Rysler, or Rycher, 8 May: the mandate addressed to Roger Damary.
15 —— John le Latimer, with the chase of Corfe: the mandate addressed to Roger Damory, 3 Dec.
18 } —— John Peche: the mandate addressed to John le
19 }   Latimer, 16 Dec.
20 —— John Mautravers.
... ... Sir John Deverel, *anno incerto*. E. II. or E. III. 4 Edw. III. he was seized and executed with Mortimer.
3 Edw. III. John Matravers, 24 Sept.
4 —— William de Montacute, together with the chase of Purbeck, 28 Dec.
13 —— Thomas Cary, as William de Montacute had it: the mandate addressed to Walter de Wydecumbe, 15 May.
15 —— Ralph de Ufford: the mandate addressed to Thomas Cary, 28 Oct.
18 —— Philip de Weston; the mandate addressed to Will. de Thway, *locum tenens* of R. de Ufford, 13 Jan.
20 —— Philip de Weston, succeeded by
20 —— Sir John Grey de Ruthyn.
33 —— Roger Mortimer, Earl of March.
36, 41, 49, Edw. III. John de Elmerugg was constable.
50 Ed. III. Bernard Brocas.
1 Ric. II. John de Arundel.
14 —— The Earl of Kent and Alice, his wife.
15 —— John Bache.
2 Edw. IV. the office of constable of our Castle of Corfe was bestowed by the King upon his brother Richard, Duke of Gloucester, " admirallum maris, &c." He was then scarcely more than ten years of age.
1 Hen. VII. Sir John Tuberville, knt., was made governor of Corfe Castle.

During the civil wars of the 17th century, Corfe Castle was rendered famous by the heroic defence made by its mistress, Lady Bankes, in the absence of her husband, when attacked by the Parliamentary forces. The following contemporary account of the seige is in the words of "Mercurius Rusticus."

"There is in the Isle of *Purbecke* a strong Castle called *Corffe Castle*, seated on a very steep hill, in the fracture of a hill, in the very midst of it, being eight miles in length, running from the east end of the Peninsula to the west; and, though it stand betweene the two ends of this fracture, so that it may seeme to lose much advantage of its naturall and artificiall strength as commanded from thence, being in height equall to, if not overlooking the tops of the highest towres of the castle, yet the structure of the castle is so strong, the ascent so steep, the walls so massie and thick, that it is one of the impregnablest forts of the kingdome, and of very great concernment, in respect of its command over the island and the places about it. This castle is now the possession and inheritance of the Right Honourable Sir John Banks, Chiefe Justice of the Common Pleas, and one of His Majesties most honourable Privy Councell, who, receiving commands from the King to attend him at Yorke in Easter Terme, 1641, had leave from the two Houses to obey those commands. After the unhappy differences betweene the King and the two Houses, or rather betweene the King and the faction in both Houses, grew high, it being generally feared that the sword would decide the controversie, the Lady Banks, a vertuous and prudent lady, resolved with her children and family to retire to this castle, there to shelter themselves from the storme which she saw comming, which accordingly she did; there she and her family remained in peace all the winter and a great part of the spring, untill May, 1643, about which time the rebels, under the command of Sir Walter Earle, Sir Thomas Trenchard, and others, had possessed themselves of Dorchester, Lyme, Melcombe, Weymouth, Warham, and Poole, (Portland Castle being treacherously delivered to the rebels) onely Corfe Castle remaining in obedience to the King; but the rebels knowing how much it concerned them to adde this castle to their other garrisons, to make all the sea-coast wholly for them, and thinking it more feizable to gain it by treachery than open hostility, rosolved to lay hold on an opportunity comming on, to see if they could become masters of it.

"There is an ancient usage that the mayor and barons (as they call them) of Corffe Castle, accompanied by the gentry of the island, have permission from the lord of the castle on May-Day to course a stagge, which every yeare is performed with much solemnity and great concourse of people. On this day some troopes of horse from Dorchester and other places came into the island, intending to find other game than to hunt the stagge, their businesse being suddenly to surprise the gentlemen in the hunting and to take the castle. The newes of their comming disperst the hunters, and spoyled the sport for that day, and made the Lady Banks to give order for the safe custodie of the castle gates, and to keep them shut against all commers. The troopers having mist their prey on the hills (the gentlemen having withdrawne themselves) some of them came to the castle under a pretence to see it, but entrance being denyed them, the common soldiers used threatning language, casting out words implying some intentions to take the castle, but the commanders (who better knew how to conceale their resolutions) utterly disavowed any such thought, denying that they had such commission; however the Lady Banks very wisely, and like her selfe, hence tooke occasion to call in a guard to assist her, not knowing how soone she might have occasion to make use of them, it being now more than probable that the rebels had a designe upon the castle. The taking in this guard, as it secured her at home, so it rendered her suspected abroad; from thence forward there was a watchfull and vigilant eye to survey all her actions; whatsoever she sends out, or sends for in, is suspected; her ordinary provisions for her family are by some multiplyed, and reported to be more than double what indeed they were, as if she had now an intention to victuall and man the castle against the forces of the two Houses of Parliament; presently letters are sent from the Committees of Poole to demand the foure small peeces in the castle, and the pretence was because the islanders conceived strange jealousies that the peeces were mounted and put on their carriages. Hereupon the Lady Banks despatched messengers to Dorchester and Poole, to entreat the commissioners that the small peeces might remain in the Castle for her own defence, and, to take away the ground of the Islanders' jealousies, she caused the peeces to be taken off their carriages againe. Hereupon a promise was made, that they should be left to her possession; but there passed not many dayes before forty seamen (they in the castle not suspecting any such thing) came very early in the morning to demand the peeces; the Lady in person (early as it was) goes to the gates and desires to see their warrant; they produce one, under the hands of some of the commissioners; but, instead of delivering them, though at that time there were but five men in the castle, yet these five, assisted by the maid-servants at their Ladies' command, mount these peeces on their carriages again, and lading one of them they gave fire, which small thunder so affrighted the sea-men that they all quitted the place and ran away. They being gone, by beat of drumme, she summons helpe into the castle, and, upon the alarme given, a very considerable guard of tenants and friends came to her assistance, there being withall some fifty armes brought into the castle, from severall parts of the island. This guard was kept in the castle about a weeke; during this time many threatening letters were sent unto the lady, telling her what great forces should be sent to fetch them, if she would not by faire meanes be perswaded to deliver them and to deprive her of her auxiliaries, all or most of them being neighbours thereabouts, they threaten that if they oppose the delivery of them they would fire their houses. Presently their wives come to the castle, there they weepe, and wring their hands, and with clamorous oratory perswade their husbands to come home, and not by saving others to expose their owne houses to spoyle and ruine: nay, to reduce the castle into a distressed condition, they did not only intercept two hundredweight of powder, provided against a seidge, but they interdict them the liberty of common markets. Proclamation is made at Warham (a market towne hard by) that no beere, beefe, or other provision should be sold to the Lady Banks, or for her use: strict watches are kept that no messenger or intelligence shall passe into or out of the castle. Being thus distressed, all means of victualling the castle being taken away, and being but slenderly furnished for a siege either with ammunition or with victuall, at last they came to a treaty of composition, of which the result was, that the Lady Banks should deliver up those 4 small peeces, the biggest carrying not above a 3 pound bullet, and that the rebels should permit her to enjoy the castle and armes in it in peace and quietnesse.

"And, though this wise lady knew too well to rest satisfied or secured in these promises (their often breach of faith having sufficiently instructed her what she might expect from them), yet she was glad of this opportunity to strengthen herselfe even by that meanes; by which many in the world thought she had done herselfe much prejudice, for the rebells, being now possessed of their guns, presumed the castle to be theirs, as sure as if they had actually possessed it. Nowe it was no more but ask and have; hereupon they grew remisse in their watches, negligent in their observations, not heeding what was brought in, nor taking care, as before, to intercept supplies which might enable them to hold out against a siege: and the Lady, making good use of their remisnes, laid hold on the present opportunity, and, as much as the time would permit, furnish't the castle with provisions of all sorts. In this intervall there was brought in a hundrede and a halfe of powder, and a quantity of match proportionable. And, understanding that the King's forces under the conduct of Prince Maurice and the Marquesse Hertford were advancing towards Blanford, she, by her messenger, made her address to them, to signifie unto them the present condition in which they were, the great consequence of the place, desiring their assistance, and in particular that they would be pleased to take into their serious consideration to send some commanders thither, to take the charge of the castle; hereupon they send Captaine Laurence, sonne of Sir Edward Laurence, a gentleman of that island, to command in chief; but he, comming without a commission, could not command moneyes or provisions to be brought in untill it was too late. There was likewise in the castle one Captaine Bond, an old souldier, whom I should deprive of his due honour not to mention him, having a share in the honour of this resistance. The first time the rebells faced the castle they brought a body of between two and three hundred horse and foot, and two peeces of ordnance, and from the hils playd on the castle, fired foure houses in the town, and then summoned the castle; but, receiving a deniall, for that time they left it. But on the three and twentieth of June, the sagacious knight Sir Walter Earle (that hath the gift of discerning treasons, and might have made up his nine and thirty treasons forty, by reckoning in his own), accompanied by Captaine Sidenham, Captaine Henry Jarvis, Captaine Skut, sonne of that arch-traytor Skut of Poole, with a body between five and six hundred, came and possessed themselves of the towne, taking the opportunity of a misty morning that they might find no resistance from the castle. They brought with them to the seige a demy-canon, a culverin, and two sacres; with these and their small shot they playd on the castle on all quarters of it, with good observation of advantages, making their battery strongest where they thought the castle weakest. And to bind the souldiers by tye of conscience to an eager prosecution of the siege, they administer them an oath, and mutually binde themselves to most unchristian resolutions, that if they found the defendants obstinate not to yield, they would maintaine the seige to victory, and then deny quarter unto all, killing without mercy men, women, and children. As to bring on their own souldiers they abused them with falshoods, telling them that the castle stood in a levell, yet with good advantages of approach, that there were but forty men in the castle, whereof twenty were for them; that there was rich booty and the like; so during the siege they used all base, unworthy meanes to corrupt the defendants to betray the castle into their hand; the better sort they endeavour to corrupt with bribes, to the rest they offer double pay, and the whole plunder of the castle. When all these arts tooke no effect, then they fall to stratagems and engines. To make their approaches to the wall with more safety, they make two engines, one they call the Sowe,* the other the Boare, being made with boards lined with wooll to dead the shot. The first that moved forward was the Sowe, but not being musket-proof she cast nine of eleven of her farrow, for the musquetiers from the castle were so good marks-men at their legs, the onely part of all their bodies left without defence, that nine ran away, as well as their broken and battered legs would give them leave, and of the two which knew neither how to run away nor well to stay, for feare, one was slaine. The Boare, of the two (a man would think) the valianter creature, seeing the ill successe of the Sowe, to cast her litter before her time, durst not advance.

The most advantageous part for their batteries was the church, which they without fear of prophanation used, not onely as their rampart, but their rendezvous. Of the surplesse they made two shirts for two souldiers, they broke downe the organs, and made the pipes serve for cases to hold their powder and shot, and, not being furnished with musquet-bullets, they cut off the lead of the church, and roll'd it up, and shoot it without ever casting in a mould. Sir Walter and the commanders were earnest to presse forward the souldiers, but, as prodigall

* This was a class of engines used as a protection for soldiers attacking a fortress. It was constructed of strong timber bound together by hoop iron, and roofed with hides and sheep-skins, to render it proof against such musket-shot or other missiles as were then in use. In front there were doors and windows which were kept closed till the walls were reached, but behind it was open for the admission or retreat of the besiegers. It was mounted on wheels, and was moved forward by the occupants by means of levers.

as they were of the blood of their common souldiers, they were sparing enough of their owne. It was a general observation, that valiant Sir Walter never willingly exposed himself to any hazard, for, being by chance endangered by a bullet, shot through his coat, afterwards he put on a beares skinne, and to the eternal honour of this knight's valour, be it recorded, for feare of musquet-shot (for other they had none) he was seen to creep on all foure on the sides of the hill, to keep himselfe out of danger. This base cowardisme in the assaylants, added courage and resolution to the defendants; therefore, not compell'd by want, but rather to brave the rebels, they sallyed out, and brought in eight cowes and a bull into the castle, without the loss of a man, or a man wounded. At another time five boyes fetcht in foure cowes. They that stood on the hills called to one in a house in the valley crying, *Shoot, Anthony*, but Anthony thought it good to sleepe in a whole skinne and durst not to looke out, so that afterwards it grew into a proverbiall jeere, from the defendants to the assaylants, *Shoot, Anthony*.

The rebels having spent much time and ammunition, and some men, and yet being as farre from hopes of taking the castle as the first day they came thither, at last the Earle of Warwicke sends them a supply of an hundred and fiftie mariners, with severall cart-loads of petars, granadoes, and other warlike provision, with scaling ladders to assault the castle by scaladoe. They make large offers to him that should first scale the wall, 20*l.* to the first, and so by descending summes a reward to the twentieth; but all this could not prevail with these silly wretches, who were brought thither, as themselves confessed, like sheep to the slaughter, some of them having but exchanged the manner of their death; the halter for the bullet, having taken them out of gaoles; one of them being taken prisoner, had letters testimoniall in his hands whence he came; the letters I meane where he was burnt for a felon being very visible to the beholders. But, when they found that perswasion could not prevaile with such abject low spirited men, the commanders resolve on another course, which was to make them drunke, knowing that drunkennesse makes some men fight like lyons, that being sober would runne away like hares. To this purpose they fill them with strong waters, even to madnesse, and ready they are now for any designe; and, for feare Sir Walter should be valiant against his will, like Cæsar, he was the onely man almost that came sober to the assault; an imitation of the Turkish practice (for certainly there can be nothing of christianity in it, to send poor soules to God's judgement seat in the very act of two grievous sins, rebellion and drunkennesse), who to stupifie their souldiers and make them insensible of their dangers, give them opium. Being now armed with drinke, they resolve to storme the castle on all sides, and apply their scaling ladders, it being ordered by the leaders (if I may, without a solecism, call them so, that stood behind and did not so much as follow), that when twenty were entred, they should give a watch-word to the rest, and that was *Old Wat;* a word ill chosen by Sir Wat. Erle, and considering the businesse in hand little better than ominous, for if I be not deceived, the hunters that beat bushes for the fearfull timorous hare, call him *Old Wat*.

"Being now pot-valiant, and possessed with a borrowed courage which was to evaporate in sleep, they divide their forces into two parties; whereof one assaults the middle ward, defended by valiant Captaine Laurence and the greater part of the souldiers; the other assault the upper ward, which the Lady Banks (to her eternall honour be it spoken) with her daughters, women, and five souldiers, undertooke to make good against the rebels, and did bravely perform what she undertooke; for by heaving over stones and hot embers, they repelled the rebels and kept them from climbing their ladders, thence to throw in that wild-fire, which every rebel had ready in his hand. Being repelled, and having in this siege and this assault lost and hurt an hundred men, *Old* Sir *Wat* hearing that the King's forces were advanced, cryed, and ran away crying, leaving Sydenham to command in chiefe, to bring off the ordnance, ammunition, and the remainder of the army; who, afraid to appeare abroad, kept sanctuary in the church till night, meaning to suppe and run away by starre-light; but, supper being ready and set on the table, an alarme was given that the King's forces were coming. This newes took away Sydenham's stomack: all this provision was but *messes of meat set before the sepulchres of the dead;* he leaves his artillery, ammunition, and (which with these men was a something) a good supper, and ran away to take boat for Poole; leaving likewise at the shore about an hundred horse, to the next takers, which next day proved good prize to the souldiers of the castle. Thus after six weeks' strict siege, this castle, the *desire* of the rebels, the *teares* of *Old* Sir *Wat*, and the *key* of those parts, by the loyalty and brave resolution of this honourable Lady, the valour of Captaine Lawrence and some eighty souldiers (by the losse only of two men), was delivered from the bloody intentions of these mercelesse rebels on the 4th of August, 1643."

It seems that the castle had been more than once attacked before the retreat of the rebels on the 4th or 5th August, 1643, for on 20th July in that year, intelligence reached the Parliament that Sir Walter Erle had besieged it a second time and had battered it with cannon, two of which were thirty-six pounders. Capt. Robert Lawrence, then a young man, only twenty-five years of age, who had already, in the first siege beat off the rebels, again made a brave resistance, killing sixty men, though he was without artillery and had less than one hundred men under his command. Sir Walter Erle, having thus failed in his attempt to take the castle, was so enraged at the valorous conduct of his adversary that, in revenge, he sent a party to Creech Grange, the residence of Sir Edward Lawrence, Capt. Lawrence's father, situated about four miles from Corfe, which they plundered and destroyed, leaving nothing but the bare walls. Lady Lawrence was forced to take refuge in the wood to save her life.*

* Mercurius Aulicus.

Clarendon relates that Lady Bankes was accompanied in the siege by some few gentlemen and tenants who betook themselves thither for her assistance and security, and that the coming of the Earl of Carnarvon had frightened Sir Walter Erle, who for a long time had besieged the castle. Sir Walter, he adds, made more haste to convey himself to London than generals used to do who have the care and charge of others.

In the accounts of the county treasurer at this time, there are some particulars relating to the foregoing transactions:

June 14, 1643, paid for loading and unloading great guns brought from Portsmouth to Corfe Castle			
June 18, paid ten soldiers for making works against the Castle			
June 26, guns brought against the castle ...			
July 7, for boards, hair, and wool, for making the sow against the castle	2	3	4
July 12, for three truckle wheels for the sow ...	0	6	0
July 10, for 74 boards and 124 feet of oaken plank employed in the siege	7	4	4
July 21, to twenty soldiers for planting the ordnance	1	0	0
July 29, for powder, match, and bullets for the gunners	268	12	3
Aug. 2, for a firkin of hot water for the soldiers when they scaled the castle...	1	12	0

Sir John Bankes died while in attendance on the king at Oxford in December following the siege, from which time, and until June, 1646, and perhaps longer, Lady Bankes, his widow, resided in London.* On the death of the Chief Justice, Corfe Castle became the property of his son and heir, Ralph, afterwards Sir Ralph Bankes, knt., and it continued to hold out for the king, being garrisoned by the royal forces. 17th May, 1645, the Committee for the Associated Western Counties gave orders to Sir Ashley Cooper for its blockade. Instructions were

* Report of the Committee of Sequestration.—See Bankes's Story of Corfe Castle, p. 225.

at the same time given to him that in case either the commander or the soldiers should be willing to surrender on composition, he was to accept such reasonable conditions as he should in his discretion think fit.* The blockade, however, must either not yet have been undertaken, or must soon have been raised; for, about 20th June, 1645, intelligence was received by the Parliament that Captain Butler, governor of Wareham, having been informed that the king's garrison at Corfe Castle had a good store of cattle, which they turned out to graze every day, but fearing the enemy, brought them into the castle every night, sent from Wareham a party of horse and foot to a place of ambush near the castle, where they laid concealed all night. In the morning, at break of day, the cattle and horses having as usual been turned out to graze, Capt. Butler, with the horse, entered the town of Corfe and approached the castle, whilst Capt. Jordan and Capt. Lawrence† attacked the enemy, and drove him into the Castle. At the same time the horse drove away the cattle from under the walls to the number of at least 140, took twenty good horses and brought them safely to Wareham, without the loss of a man.‡

In Oct., 1645, after Bristol was taken, there was no longer any garrison between Exeter and London, which held out for the king except Corfe, which was then straitly blockaded by the governor of Pool and by Col. Pickering's regiment, sent there for that purpose.§

23rd Dec., 1645. Sir Thomas Fairfax received intelligence of the enemy's intention to march with their army to relieve Exeter, and of their preparations and provisions to that end, and on 25th Dec., or thereabouts, he was informed by the committee of both kingdoms of an incursion made by the king's horse from Oxford into the adjacent parts, doing much mischief thereto; whereupon the regiment of Col. Rainsborough, then before Corfe Castle, was commanded to march thence to Abingdon.‖

* Shaftesbury Papers at Wimborne St. Giles.
† This must have been Capt. Richard Lawrence, of Winterborn Steepleton, in this county, who "was an active man for the Parliament."
‡ Vincint's Parl. Chron. The Burning Bush, pp. 174-5.
§ Sprigg, p. 145.   ‖ Ibid, p. 161.

16th Dec., a regiment of horse and two of foot were sent by Sir Thomas Fairfax to assist in the siege of Corfe.*

14th Feb., 1645-6, a troop of the king's forces, consisting of about 120 men, under Col. Cromwell, came into Dorsetshire to relieve Corfe Castle, and marched through Col. Cooke's quarters undiscovered. At Wareham they told the sentinels that they were a troop of Fairfax's horse, and being admitted into the town they went straight to the house of Col. Butler, the governor, who, recognising their true character, shut his door, and with his son fired on them, and defended his house for three hours. Then the enemy fired the house, which, being near the magazine, the governor was forced to yield. They carried Col. Butler and two committee men prisoners to Corfe Castle, the Parliament's forces retiring at their approach, though four times as many as those in the fortress. Then some of the royalists returned to Wareham to assist the new governor, but Col. Cooke beat them out of the town, and took their commander-in-chief, together with seven prisoners. After this, Col. Butler, being prisoner in Corfe Castle, contrived to make his escape, together with Colonel Lawrence, who having hitherto gallantly supported the royal cause, as appears above, had now resolved to join the Parliament, and both of them got out together.†

No very formidable attack on the castle seems to have been made since the first siege, and it is by no means improbable that its impregnable position and the comparative weakness in those days of the enemy's artillery, might have enabled it to preserve its independence till the whole nation had succumbed to the revolution. Nothing indeed but famine or treachery could subdue it, and the latter, as the most easy means, was ultimately had recourse to. The following is an account of its final surrender in a letter from a person whose name is not mentioned, but who is described as a trustworthy correspondent in the neighbourhood. He writes as if he had personal knowledge of the facts he relates:—

* Whitelock. † Whitelock's Memorials, 2nd ed., p. 192.

"There being in Corfe Castle one Lieut.-Colonel Pitman, who had formerly served under Lord Inchequin in Ireland; upon some intimation given that he had a desire to do the Parliament acceptable service in procuring this castle to be delivered up to the Parliament's possession, in case he might have a protection granted him. Accordingly a protection was here privately procured and sent down unto him; thereupon the plot was laid, viz., Lieut.-Colonel Pitman having speech with Captain Aniketel, (Anketil) the governor, told him that if he would give way unto it he would go into Somersetshire and privately get one hundred men more and bring them unto the castle, and then, considering what had been formerly done, he made no question but they should beat off the besiegers, and make them quit the place, and he would find means to colour his going out by obtaining leave to go for an exchange of a friend of his for one of the Parliament side that was prisoner in the castle; which being assented unto and leave being given by Col. Bingham,* for him to go forth accordingly, an appointment was made, and the design so laid as that Pitman, under colour of bringing in the 100 men for the enemy, should bring in 100 of the Parliament's soldiers, and that the besiegers should give the onset the same time. Accordingly, 100 commanded men were taken out of the several companies of the garrison of Weymouth, and secretly marched to Lulworth Castle, whence they marched away, with some thirty or forty more joined with them, as silently as they could, until they came to the place, Lieut.-Col. Pitman leading them on to the sally-port, where Capt. Aniketil, the governor, stood to welcome them with much courtesy. Some of the men being Somersetshire men, fitted for the purpose—he being that countryman—yet some intermixed amongst them in a disguised habit who knew all parts of the castle. When fifty of these were entered, Captain Aniketel, seeing so many yet behind, refused to suffer any more to enter, saying those were enough and more than he could tell what to do with, at which

---

* He was in command of the besieging forces.

Pitman seemed to be very angry, saying he had done him wrong in causing him to bring men so far with the hazard of their lives, and then to shut them out and make them lie in the cold, and be in danger of having their throats cut. But those that were taken in got presently some of them into the King's tower, others into the Queen's tower, and the rest into the two platforms, standing upon their guard, and making it good, expecting the besiegers would give the onset by escalado or otherwise, it being about two of the clock after midnight, and thus it continued three or four hours, the besiegers in all that time never falling on, and the gunners in the mean space shooting (shouting?) and vapouring, and threatening to cut the throats of all that were entered. But these fifty stood stoutly to it. At last, when it was open day, the besiegers, when they saw their friends that were formerly entered to be on the top of the towers and platforms, then they began to show themselves, and the enemy bestowed some shot on them, but without doing harm. At last the garrison, seeing themselves betrayed, and that it was bootless for them to stand out any longer, demanded a parley, which was granted, the agreement made that all their lives should be spared, and those that were of the town should return quietly to their houses. Whereupon two, by a ladder, came over the wall, the rest seeing it began to shoot, and so broke quarter. So, in conclusion, they all became prisoners at discretion, their lives excepted, being seven score in number or thereabouts. The soldiers got store of plunder, besides which there were found seventeen barrels of powder, with matches, &c., good store of victuals, besides thirty prisoners or thereabouts set at liberty. In this action there was but one man lost on the Parliament side, though the enemy shot often, and threw down great stones from the castle walls. And thus," adds the writer who records this letter, " the Lord every way mightily showed himself for us, to the glory of his own great name, the good of us his unworthy servants, and the great dread and amazement of all our implacable and incorrigible enemies. To Him, therefore, alone be all the honour and glorie of these our most memorable mercies and mighty deliverances."*

Mr. Denis Bond, who resided near Corfe, and kept a chronology, alludes very briefly to this event, which must have been of stirring interest in the neighbourhood. He merely says, "Corfe Castle, in the Isle of Purbeck, was delivered up by Col. Pitman, of Somerset, into the hands of the Parliament, 27th Feb., 1645"; but according to the Microchronicon the surrender took place on the 26th. Whitelock says the news was received on the 27th, but Vincent gives the 28th as the date of its reception.

In Sprigg's table of battles and sieges, the siege of Corfe Castle is said to have lasted 48 days, during which twenty men were slain, and five pieces of ordnance were taken.

5th March, 1645-6, the House of Commons ordered £10 to be bestowed on the captain that gave the news of the taking of Corfe Castle, and £10 on the messenger that brought the news thereof.†

On the same day a vote passed the House of Commons to demolish Corfe Castle.‡

The decree of the Parliament was ruthlessly carried into effect, and far more was unfortunately done than was sufficient to render the castle utterly untenable for the future. Most of the towers were undermined, while others had the soil removed from the foundation, preparatory to a similar process. Some were blown up with gunpowder, which must have been used in enormous quantities, whilst others, perhaps, sunk down by their own weight into the mines, without the aid of that mighty and irresistible agent.

Captain Hughes, the governor of Lulworth Castle, was employed in the destruction, and in his disbursements he

---

* Vincent's Parliamentary Chronicle. The Burning Bush Consumed. Whitelock in his Memorials, 2nd ed., p. 192, gives a paraphrase of the above, apparently derived from there.

† Journal of the House of Commons.

‡ Ibid. Hutchins, following Whitelock, says the house ordered it to be "slighted," but "demolish" is the word used in the vote as recorded in the journal.

charges £200 for taking down the materials of the castle by agreement with the committee of the county; and he also accounts for £141 13s. 8d. borrowed for the same purpose. Besides this. £26 13s. 4d. appears in his account as having been paid for wood out of Grange farm. It is difficult to see how this wood could have been utilised for the purpose unless the timber was employed for propping the buildings during the process of undermining, whilst brushwood may have been used to fire the props, and thus permit the super-incumbent masses of masonry to sink down into the mines.

The rebels not only plundered the castle, dividing among them its sumptuous furniture, some of which was traced by Sir Ralph Bankes, after the restoration, to the houses of county gentlemen, and some to dealers in London, but even timber and stone were found to have been appropriated by some gentlemen of the county who supported the cause of the Parliament. Most of the lead was sold to a plumber of Poole. The soldiers either set or followed the example, and the shop goods of the loyal tradesmen of the town of Corfe were amongst the loot which they seized for their own use.*

We obtain a glimpse of the disturbance of social life, produced by these events, in a petition to Parliament, by one Richard Brine, a tradesman of the town of Corfe, dated 14 Nov., 1645. He complains that in May, 1643, Lady Bankes, living in Corfe Castle, began to raise a garrison against the Parliament and collected and maintained at her own charge eighty men, or more, completely armed, and also procured a gunner for the castle. By these means the whole island was ruined and the county brought into subjection to the king's forces. Petitioner affirms that being an inhabitant of the town of Corfe and more cordially for the Parliament than other men, he has been utterly undone by the garrison, who had taken away his goods to the value of £200,

---

* Letter of Edward Harvey, a Corfe tradesman, written to Sir Ralph Bankes, 5 Oct., 1660. See Bankes's Story of Corfe Castle, p. 249.

pulled down two of his houses in the town and carried the stones into the castle to annoy the besiegers. He thereupon prays that he may receive satisfaction for his losses out of the estate of Lady Bankes.*

Another instance may be cited which, though it did not actually occur at Corfe, took place in the immediate neighbourhood, and was probably associated with some of the events above related.

In 1654, a petition was presented to the Protector from the inhabitants of Stoborough, in which they allege that in 1643 they willingly permitted their "town" of one hundred families to be burned, to preserve the Parliament garrison of Wareham, when the king's forces were most prevalent in the county, and thus they lost £3,000 and were ruined. They add that they had been unwilling to trouble the state till the troubles were over, but they had then addressed themselves to Cromwell and were referred to the Parliament, whose multiplied business would not admit debate on private affairs. They therefore now addressed themselves to the Protector. This petition was referred to the Council 9 June, 1655.†

The destruction of such a building as Corfe Castle must ever be a subject of universal regret. But it is likewise deeply to be lamented that what was partially effected by the hand of man, time, and the elements, are now gradually completing. Year by year the ruined walls continue to crumble away. Large masses of masonry have fallen even within living memory, and every gale of wind throws down and disperses the loosened stones. Thus many interesting features continue to perish. This gradual decay, however, is aided by the inordinate growth of ivy, which, while it conceals many interesting details, is gradually and stealthily sapping the walls.

---

* Appendix to sixth report of Historical M.S., Commission, 1877, p. 84.
† Calendar of State papers. Domestic, 1655, p. 211.

GENERAL DESCRIPTION.

The district called the Isle of Purbeck, of which the little town of Corfe is the metropolis, is situated in the south-east corner of Dorsetshire and is in fact no more than a peninsula. It extends nearly twelve miles from east to west and nine miles from north to south. It is bounded by the sea on the south and east, and also partly on the south-west; by the Poole estuary and the river Frome on the north; and on the greatest part of the west by a small rivulet called Luckford Lake, which, rising at West Whiteway, in Tyneham parish, flows into the Frome near West Holme. A line drawn from the source of this stream to the ancient earthworks on the summit of the hill at Flowersbarrow, overhanging Worbarrow Bay, crosses the isthmus which connects Purbeck with the mainland of the county.

The Isle is divided into two nearly equal parts by a lofty ridge of chalk hills, rising abruptly on either side to the height, on one part, of more than six hundred feet and running in a gentle curve from Flowersbarrow to the bluff headland called Handfast Point on the north side of Swanage bay. The only opening in this range of hills, except at Ulwell, near its eastern extremity, is about midway between its two ends. Here the continuity of the range has, by the operation of nature, been completely severed, leaving in the midst of the opening a portion of the chalk formation, which assumes the shape of a nearly isolated precipitous hill of an irregular triangular form, connected only at its southern apex with the lower table-land adjoining. To this remarkable opening the Anglo-Saxons gave the appropriate name of "Corvensgeat" or "Corvesgate" derived from a combination of their words "ceorfan," to cut, and "geat," a gate. It is in fact one of nature's gigantic cuttings, and forms the gateway or pass by which access is obtained from the northern part of the island to the secluded valley of Purbeck.

The base of this isolated hill is almost surrounded by two small streams, anciently called the Wicken stream and Byle brook, which, uniting on the north-east side, flow on as one to the estuary of Poole. The narrow isthmus which originally united the southern angle of the castle hill to the adjoining table land on which the town of Corfe now stands, has been cut through by the hand of man, and on the summit of the hill, thus isolated by nature and art, stands the majestic ruin hereafter described.

Whether Corfe Castle is regarded in association with some striking passages in history, or as an example of mediæval military architecture, or simply as a picturesque object, it is equally interesting.

The Foss above mentioned which separates the castle from the town of Corfe is spanned by a lofty and substantial stone bridge of four arches, about one hundred feet long, by twenty feet broad. It is probably of no very high antiquity in its present form in comparison with the works of the castle itself, though its masonry, which is totally devoid of mouldings and other distinctive features, affords but slight evidence of its date, for the excellence of its workmanship and the high preservation of its materials are equalled if not excelled by the more ancient buildings of the castle. There is no parapet, the arches are nearly semicircular and of different dimensions, with buttresses between them, the widest arch being 17 feet 10 inches, and the narrowest 9 feet 11 inches, whilst their

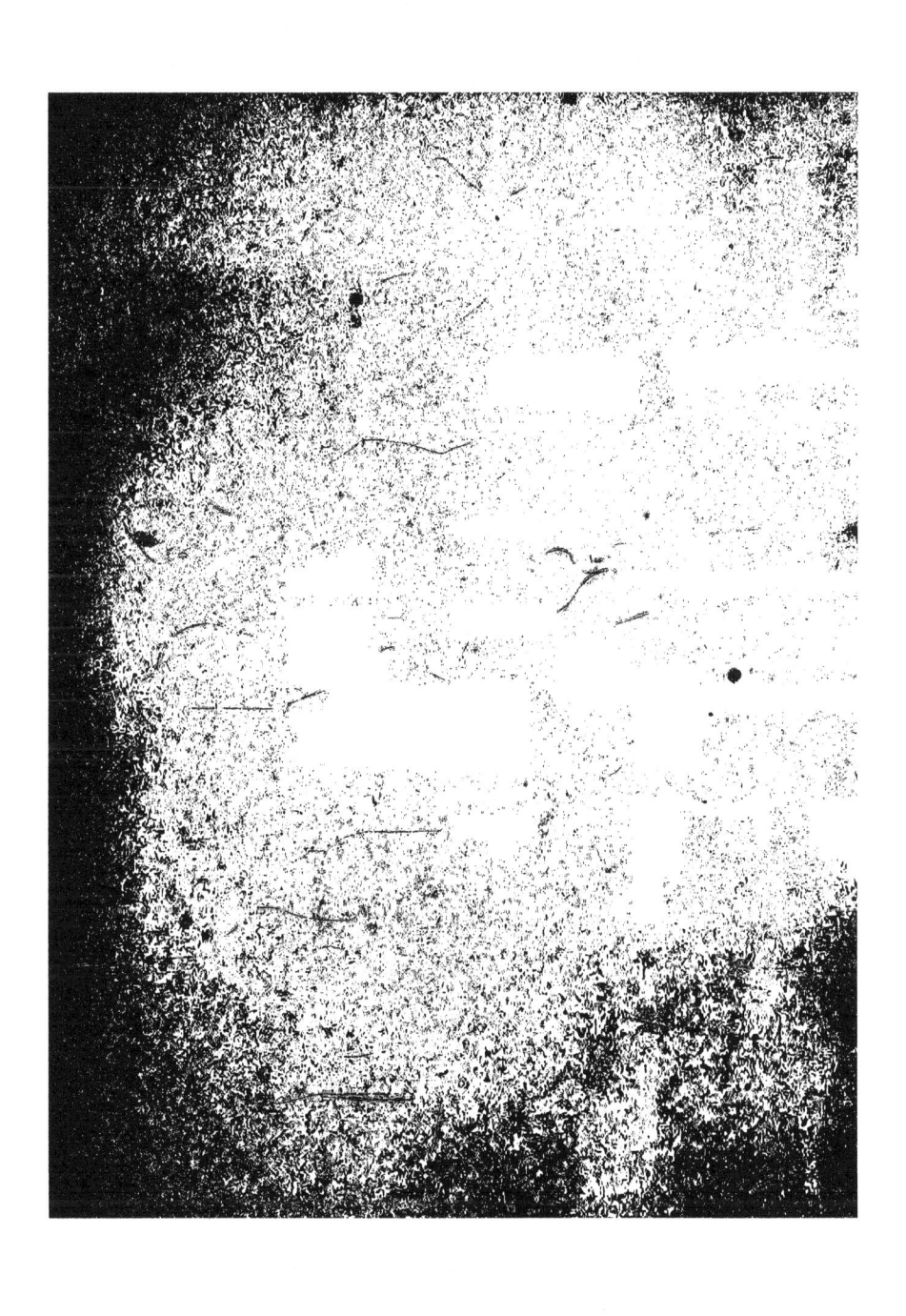

CORFE CASTLE.

South View from the Church Tower.

DESCRIPTION.

, that of the centre one being about 25 feet from the present level of the ground.

There can be no doubt that between the north end of and the castle gate, a space of about 25 feet, there was originally a draw-bridge, but the earth has been filled in, and no traces of it now remain.

The plan of the castle is adapted to the shape of the hill on which it stands, its outer walls following and the crest of the hill. The surface of the hill has formed, partly by nature and partly by art, into three platforms rising one above the other, each of which separately fortified, formed, as it were, a distinct fortress. highest of these platforms occupies the north-east angle hill, and is separated by a steep grassy cliff or escarp from the southern or lowest portion which is wholly by the outer ward. The original castle was no limited to this elevated spot, and here consequently we with its earliest remains.

 destruction of the castle must have been effected by explosion of gunpowder and partly by merely . All the towers bear evidence of the earth having removed from their foundations with the intention of them down, while some, it is equally clear, have ly undermined.

THE FIRST WARD OR OUTER BAILEY.

The entrance gateway is flanked by a pair of massive drum towers about twenty feet in diameter. They are solid masses of masonry as high as the crown of the arch which united . Resting on this solid base were apartments now destroyed. In each of them were three loops or slits for discharging arrows which the French approly call "meurtrières." There were three more in the immediately over the archway, the lower ends which are still discernible. Both these towers have been

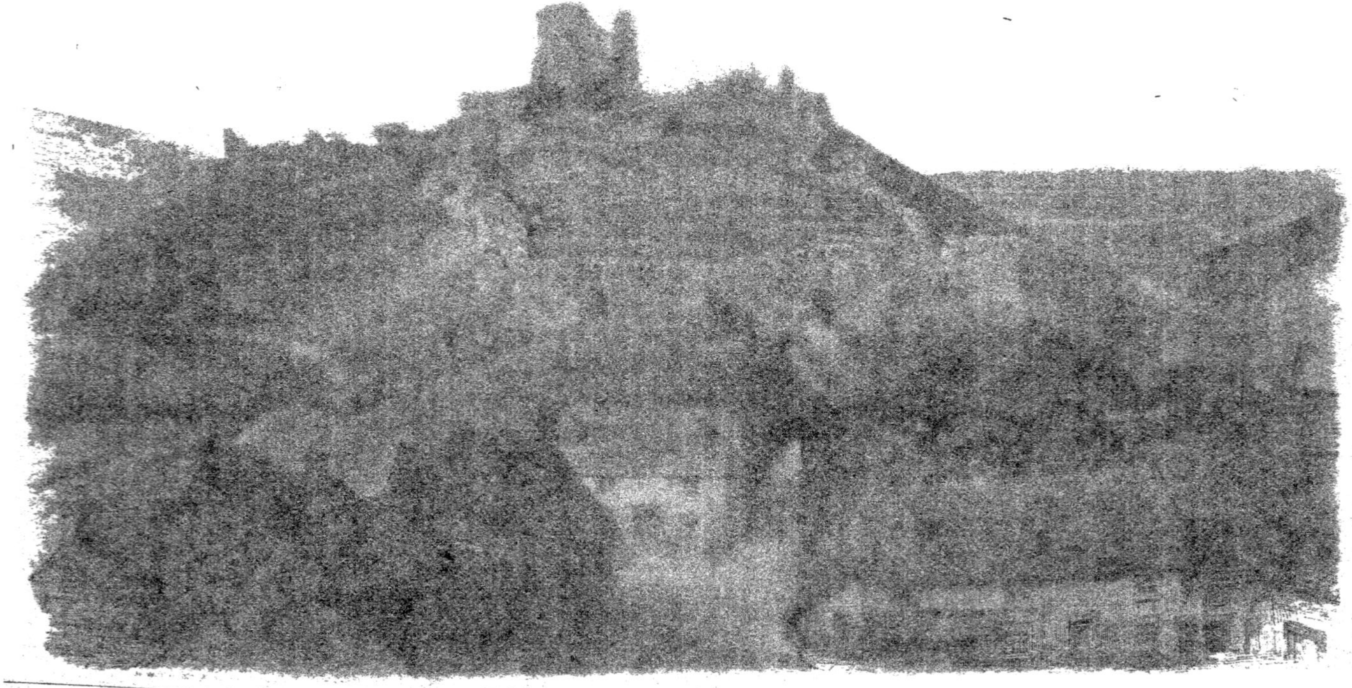

height is also unequal, that of the centre one being about 25 feet from the present level of the ground.

There can be no doubt that between the north end of the bridge and the castle gate, a space of about 25 feet, there was originally a draw-bridge, but the earth has been filled in, and no traces of it now remain.

The plan of the castle is adapted to the shape of the ground on which it stands, its outer walls following and crowning the crest of the hill. The surface of the hill has been formed, partly by nature and partly by art, into three distinct platforms rising one above the other, each of which being separately fortified, formed, as it were, a distinct fortress. The highest of these platforms occupies the north-east angle of the hill, and is separated by a steep grassy cliff or escarpment from the southern or lowest portion which is wholly embraced by the outer ward. The original castle was no doubt limited to this elevated spot, and here consequently we meet with its earliest remains.

The destruction of the castle must have been effected partly by explosion of gunpowder and partly by merely undermining. All the towers bear evidence of the earth having been removed from their foundations with the intention of throwing them down, while some, it is equally clear, have been actually undermined.

THE FIRST WARD OR OUTER BAILEY.

The entrance gateway is flanked by a pair of massive drum towers about twenty feet in diameter. They are solid masses of masonry as high as the crown of the arch which united them. Resting on this solid base were apartments now wholly destroyed. In each of them were three loops or narrow slits for discharging arrows which the French appropriately call "*meurtrières.*" There were three more in the connecting wall, immediately over the archway, the lower ends of which are still discernable. Both these towers have been undermined and forced from their perpendicular position. That on the left hand has sunk down into the mine, and, falling forward, has rent asunder the archway which spanned the entrance. This rent has been needlessly built up within living memory.

The outer arch of the gateway is of semicircular form. It springs out of the wall, is unsupported by jambs or corbels, and has neither mouldings nor ornament of any kind. Immediately within it is a machicolation or narrow opening in the vaulting overhead, about a foot wide, for throwing down missiles on the besiegers. Behind this, and in front of the jambs of the gate is, on either wall, a carefully executed circular groove about 9 inches in diameter, and 7 inches opening, the use of which, on account of its unusual form, has been a matter of some doubt amongst antiquaries. But it is in the position usually occupied by a portcullis, and it is difficult to conceive what other purpose it could have served. Excepting this, there are no other indications of a portcullis in the gateway, and it is in the highest degree improbable that the principal entrance to such a fortress as this would have been left without a method of defence universally adopted.

Immediately behind this the gates were hung. The jambs alone remain, the arch which united them having been destroyed. This arch was segmental in form, with but little rise, and was equally plain with the outer one before described. The whole of the passage was arched with stone.

Just within the gateway, on either side, are remains of the rooms shown in Treswell's plan,* both of them having remains of chimneys.

The court of the warrener was held weekly in an apartment at the castle gate, and other apartments were no doubt appropriated to the use of the porter and the guard. Till very recently some small remains of a newel stairs were distinguishable on the right side leading to the apartments over the gateway.

* See Ground Plan at the end of the volume.

Passing through the great gateway we enter the first ward, or base court, the "*ballivum forinsecum*," or outer bailey, a spacious area overlooked by the great tower, dungeon, or keep, which rises majestically from the steep escarpment immediately opposite. The whole of this ward with its two gateways, excepting the north-eastern tower and perhaps the curtain wall, adjacent to it on either side, seems to have been built by King Edward 1., as will appear hereafter under the head of "The Fabric." Besides the gateway towers, this ward contains six others of semicircular form, five of them being now quite open towards the ward. They were intended merely for defence, not for habitation. All of them, except the north-eastern one, but including those of the two gateways, are beautiful examples of masonry. They are faced with ashlar, accurately worked and closely jointed, and the material remains in perfect preservation. All rest externally on projecting plinths.* The curtains are of rougher material, and the core of the walls throughout the whole castle is formed of chalk and rubble, grouted together with liquid mortar, and is of extraordinary strength and solidity. So excellent, indeed, is the mortar, that in some places it has actually proved more durable than the stone itself. Each of the towers of this ward, except that on the south-west, has narrow perpendicular slits or loops, through which arrows were discharged. They are about an inch and a-half wide, and about seven feet long, with a downward rake, and are generally three in number, two of them raking the curtain, the other directed towards the field. In the south-western tower of this ward, as well as a solitary one in the inner tower of the second gateway, all the loops are cruciform.

Turning to the right, after entering the great gate, the curtain wall connecting it with the south-east tower is found

---

* The stone used is locally known by the name of Bur, and it is perhaps the most durable building stone in England. The vein is fonnd near the base of the southern range of hills, and runs from one end of the island to the other, but is of no great thickness. The ashlar here used has been occasionally adjusted and wedged up by bits of slate which from the colour seem to be French.

to be about eight feet six inches thick, and adjoining this tower are remains of a small vaulted chamber, about six feet wide, with a narrow window in the corner looking towards the ward. The head of the doorway is formed by overlapping stones in lieu of an arch. This tower exhibits joist holes in the masonry, as if floors had at one time rested there, and though it cannot be determined at what period this was so, the original and still open front may possibly at some time or other have been inclosed by a brattice of wood or other unsubstantial kind of construction.

Proceeding northwards, the walls on this side the ward are only from six feet eight inches to seven feet three inches thick. The castle hill being extremely precipitous, a lesser strength of wall here than elsewhere was no doubt deemed to be sufficient. This wall shows the lower ends of loops, about eighteen feet apart, which must have been served by archers on the summit of the wall behind the battlements. They are so constructed as to rake down the steep face of the hill, but do not command the curtains.

The stable shown in Treswell's plan, which stood between the south-east and north-east towers is entirely destroyed, and much of the outer wall here has perished. About midway between the stable and the last mentioned tower, something has been destroyed and built up again, the site being now partially obscured by bushes. It might, perhaps, have been a sally-port.

The north-eastern tower is of different masonry and construction from the others in the same ward, and so, perhaps, is the eastern curtain, and they seem to be of earlier date. This tower is semicircular within, and is faced with rather rude ashlar, being straight on the outside from top to bottom, without any plinth or base like the other towers. In the upper part of its outer face is sculptured in bold relief a shield held up by two human hands issuing from the wall, and charged, as an heraldic device, with five fusils in bend. It is the only object throughout the castle which can be regarded as in the nature of a date. The arms are in all probability those of Alan de Plunkenet, who was constable of the castle in 1269, 54th Hen. III., and they afford an example of the utility of heraldry as an ornament. Further mention of this shield will be met with when we treat hereafter of "The Fabric" of the castle.

Close to the north side of the tower just described there was a newel stairs, constructed partly in the thickness of the wall and partly in an angle projecting beyond its outer face, but now almost wholly destroyed. It led up to the battlements, and *chemin de ronde*, of this part of the external wall, which here rose rapidly towards the north, till it reached the fortifications of the inner castle. It meets the building at its northern end at an angle which seems to require explanation, because it leaves a portion of the castle hill outside the walls sufficiently level for an enemy to make use of it in attacking the upper work, whereas everywhere else the works are placed on the very brow of the hill. My idea is that this wall originally extended farther north, across the site of the present most western buildings of the inner ward, and when these buildings were erected and carried forward to the brink of the hill, the earth being perhaps in some measure artificially formed for the purpose, the only part of this wall which was allowed to remain was that which is now partially standing. This wall is of quite a different construction from the other curtain walls of this ward, its stones being squared and coursed, forming a rather rude ashlar. A small portion of a corbel table, with corbels of a very simple character, still remains at its interior summit. This wall is, no doubt, of earlier date than those to which it adjoins, and may possibly be of the Norman period. At its point of junction with the more recent wall next the stairs above mentioned, a straight jamb in the masonry shows that it extended no farther in that direction, but from its section it is apparent that it turned nearly at right angles, and ran diagonally athwart the site of the present ditch, probably sweeping round the base of the hill on which the keep is placed, and which, in its original form, may have swelled out into the present ward. Returning to the great gateway, some traces may be seen near its western side of an external stairs which led to the summit of the walls.

On the western side of this ward are four mural semicircular towers, unlike, in some respects, those on the opposite side, as they are angular within instead of semicircular, as are the others. The curtain wall which connects the great gateway with the first of these towers on the south-west side of the ward is ten feet nine inches thick above the plinth, which is one foot nine inches more, making the whole thickness of the foundation twelve feet one inch. The southwest tower just mentioned, though built on a solid foundation 26 feet wide, has been forced from its original position by the explosion of gunpowder, having been first undermined, and the large fragment of it which remains leans over the precipice as if about to topple down into the stream below. It is angular within, and it had three cruciform loops, its foundation being perforated by a drain.

A little northward of this, and adjoining the curtain, was a gardrobe, of which no traces remain except of the vault. Much of the curtain wall on this side of the ward has been displaced, one large fragment near the gardrobe has been so completely overthrown that it now rests on what was its outer face. Another large portion has been forced forward about three feet, and leans considerably towards the west. Very near the second tower was a well, protected by a well-house, some vestiges of which can be discerned.

Nearly adjoining the last-named tower are the remains of a small doorway, the jambs of which are about four feet within the outer face of the wall. It looks like a postern, or sally-port, but it is not shown in Treswell's plan.

The third tower on this side seems to have been partially closed at the gorge, all the others being entirely open to the ward. Each of the two last-named towers has three simple loops, one of them being directed towards the field, the others raking the curtain. The fourth mural tower has a little stone shelf, or locker, in the inside, similar to that at the opposite end of the fosse and has also three loops; the one directed towards the field is normal in character, but on the south side are two, one above the other, one being of very unusual character. The lower one, while shorter than the others, turns at a right angle at its summit and is carried on a little further in a horizontal direction. Just above this is another, of the ordinary form, but very short. There is at present none towards the north, the tower of the second gateway being but little in advance of it.

The curtain which unites the last-mentioned mural tower to the adjacent gateway tower is peculiar. It is built across the fosse, which is here carried on outside the castle and some way down the face of the hill. The masonry is quite unlike that of the adjacent walls, or indeed that of any other part of the castle. It is rough, and indifferently executed, and the put-lug holes for scaffolding have never been filled in. It is only about four feet six inches thick above the base, which is about two feet more.

It has four long loops, wider than was usual for archers, placed high above the ground so that it is not easy to see how they could have been made use of unless by means of a wooden platform in the inside. It is evidently of more recent date than the adjoining tower, for an older and more carefully constructed wall once occupied its site. This is apparent from a small fragment of the latter adjoining the base of the tower on its outside. The masonry of this fragment corresponds, and appears to have been built contemporaneously, with the tower to which it is worked in, and differs widely from that of the existing curtain; the latter looks as if it had been hastily constructed. This was perhaps about the weakest point in the whole *enceinte* of the walls, and here therefore it is natural to look for greater rather than inferior strength of fortification.

The outer ward is separated from the inner works of the castle by a deep dry moat or fosse, cut in the solid rock at the base of the steep escarpment, which is crowned by the dungeon or keep, and by the other buildings of the upper castle. It commences at the east curtain wall, and being dug down below the level of its foundation, it passes the second gateway, and is carried out beyond the western curtain, till it vanishes on the side of the hill. The chalk and earth thrown out from it has been formed into four terraces on one of which, in the 16th century, small pieces of ordnance were mounted.

A second bridge of two arches crosses the fosse and leads to the second gateway. It is very similar to the outer bridge already described, and, like the latter, it originally terminated in a draw-bridge crossing a space now filled up, of about eighteen feet in length, adjoining the portal. The piers of this bridge look as if they were of earlier date than the arches which span them. They have holes in the masonry which may, perhaps, have served for fixing the timber work of an earlier wooden bridge.

The second gateway is much like the first, except that while the front of the right-hand tower is semicircular, the sides are flat and parallel. The gateway is a very imposing structure. The masonry is admirably executed, and the ashlar is in perfect preservation. But unfortunately, some of its most interesting features are wholly concealed from view by a dense coating of luxurious ivy. The annexed wood-cut is copied from a photograph fortunately taken before the ivy had acquired its present blinding dimensions. It exhibits the corbel stones near the summit, which supported a wooden hoard, intended to protect the defenders of the gateway while throwing down missiles on the heads of the besiegers. The groove for the portcullis, which is cut with extreme precision, is here of the usual semicircular form; but the machicolations are placed between the portcullis and the gate. A second portcullis, a little farther on, and within the gate, gave additional security to the second ward, in the event of the former being the first to fall into the hands of the enemy. The western tower of this gateway served also as a mural tower, and having, like others of the mural towers, been undermined, it has sunk down bodily into the mine below, nearly the whole height of its lower chamber, and, though thrust forward about six feet into the fosse, it has almost retained its perpendicular position. The walls and archways which united it to its companion tower have thus been riven asunder; but so admirable is the masonry, so tenacious the mortar, that its surface has

suffered no injury. Its lower apartment has three loops, and must have been rather low, as the floor above it was immediately over the entrance doorway. The joists of the floor above it, which were very stout, were let into the wall on one side, and rested on a set-off on the other, showing that the practice was to finish the masonry first, and add the carpenters' work afterwards. The upper apartment of the tower must have been quite dark, and was probably an *oubliette* entered by a trap door from the floor above, for it has neither door nor window, and was no doubt used as a prison.

The right-hand tower of this gateway is built partly within the fosse, and springs from about half its depth. Probably a good deal of it is buried in rubbish. A close examination of its masonry, so far as the blinding ivy will permit, seems to disclose that it was built at a different time from the curtain which connects it with the great tower. It has a low apartment on the ground floor, with only a single cruciform loop, now quite hidden by ivy, but which raked the bridge. This apartment was entered by a doorway without an arch, but surmounted by a discharging arch. In one corner of it is the matrix of a newel stair, which led to the upper story, and thence to a narrow flight of steps on the summit of the curtain wall, ascending to the great tower.* The chamber on the first floor of this tower has a fire-place, and in the room above it a square-headed window has been inserted and again stopped up.

THE SECOND WARD, OR MIDDLE BAILEY.

Passing through the gateway just described, we enter the second ward, which occupies a platform more elevated than the last. It is approached by a narrow roadway, having on the left a fragment of the curtain wall, here only five feet three inches thick, crowning the brow of the hill, and on the right is a steep chalk acclivity which supports the keep and the more recent work called the "New Bulwark." The chalk has been partially cut away to form this road, which is completely commanded by the works above it. Even after the second gateway had fallen into the hands of the besiegers this narrow passage could be defended.

The whole area of this ward, which is triangular in form, has been greatly modified, for the ground originally sloped rapidly from the upper platform towards the western extremity of the hill. The earth and chalk have at different times

---

* This has been sometimes erroneously called the great staircase. It was, in fact, simply a continuation of the usual *chemin de ronde*, or passage which ran round the summit of the whole of the outer walls of the castle, inside the battlements; but owing to the position of this wall, which is built up the steep side of the hill, it has assumed the form of stairs.

been moved — much of it no doubt since the outer works were built — and two distinct platforms have been made, one of which is considerably below the level of the other.

In this ward are the remains of two half-round mural towers and of one of octagonal form. These, with the exception of the bases of the former, are not faced with ashlar, and their masonry a good deal resembles that of the north-east tower of the outer ward, though rather superior in execution. They were evidently constructed at a somewhat earlier period than most of those of the outer bailey.

The first tower on the left hand, which is reached after entering this ward, had the usual three loops. It has been almost wholly destroyed, and its base, which alone remains, has been torn from the adjoining curtain, and has sunk down somewhat below its original level. A small apartment, with a fire-place, has been made within it, apparently since its destruction. This was approached through another, obviously of the same date, of which the foundations only now remain, measuring thirteen feet by eleven.

This tower was never entirely open on the inside next the ward, like most of the other mural towers of the castle. It was partially built up against the outside of a far more ancient wall, constructed in the peculiar style of masonry commonly known as "herringbone work." The stones of this work are flat and thin, and are set on edge, inclining diagonally. They are so arranged that the stones of each course incline inversely to those of the courses above and below. The quoin which terminated the eastern end of this herringbone wall has been pulled down, and the wall has been extended in masonry of an ordinary character across the gorge of the tower, with a doorway in the midst leading to the inner apartment before mentioned.

A curtain wall, about seven feet six inches thick, has been built up outside and against the herringbone wall, and extends westwards from the mural tower last described, till it joins another tower of octagonal shape, crowning the extreme western spur of the castle hill, and which, from its prominent situation, was denominated the "Butavant" tower. Where this outer wall quits the first mentioned tower, a single battlement remains, the only one left standing in the castle.

The herringbone wall ceases about twenty-six feet ten inches short of the Butavant and is about three feet three inches thick, so that, as far as it extends, the two combined walls measure ten feet eight inches in thickness. The herringbone wall is constructed in similar style in both its faces, and originally measured from end to end about seventy-one feet, inside measure. It had three small windows, about equidistant from each other, two of which are still perfect, though one of them has been wholly, and the other partly, built up with masonry. The third is partially destroyed. They are of similar form and size. The opening of the windows was six inches in width and about two feet six inches in height, but they are splayed within to two feet in width and four feet six inches in height. The windows are square-headed, but the splays carry semicircular arches, the whole being neatly executed in ashlar. The two outer windows of the three are each about equi-distant, viz., about eighteen feet, from the respective ends of the building.

The peculiar character of this wall, and its extremely weatherbeaten appearance indicate great antiquity, and render it worthy of special notice. It evidently could not have originally formed part of the military defences of the castle, and it must therefore be a fragment of some building of either an ecclesiastical or civil character.

With a view to ascertain, if possible, what was the nature and purpose of the building of which this fragment once formed a part, I have, by permission of the owner, searched for foundations, commencing at the west end of the existing wall, where a section shows that it originally turned at right angles. At four feet below the turf the set-off of the ancient foundation was reached, and following its course, the whole was laid open to its full extent. At the distance of nearly twenty-two feet from the corner where the section is seen, the foundation turns again, and runs parallel to the existing wall to about the same length as the latter, and then turning again at right angles, it met the southern wall near its present termination. The set-off of the foundation at the east end, where there is no superstructure, is about six feet wide; elsewhere it is less, the width of what remains of the wall itself being about three feet three inches. Buttresses about three feet eight inches wide, and projecting about ten and a-half inches, terminated the west ends of both the north and south walls, but there is no appearance of there having been any in the lateral walls. The height of the herringbone wall towards the west end is eleven feet above the turf, and four feet four inches below it, making fifteen feet four inches in all. It was no doubt once somewhat higher. The left-hand jamb of a doorway is apparent in the northern foundation at fourteen feet nine inches from the face of the buttress. Fragments of herringbone work here and there show that the whole building was constructed in the same fashion both inside and out. No indication was met with in the masonry that there were ever any original cross walls, neither are there any original joist holes, which might have shown that the building had contained two or more stories. Additional evidence that there never was an upper story is found in the position of the single row of windows. The sill of the western one seems to have been about ten feet five inches above the set-off of the foundation, but that near the other extremity is about seven feet ten inches above it. At about twenty-seven feet nine inches eastward from the outside of the west wall is a comparatively recent cross wall, three feet three inches thick, which, leaping over a fragment of the herringbone, here six feet six inches high, is crrried on northwards some way outside the older word. An excavation to the foundation of this cross wall seems to show that three successive walls have been built at different times on this spot; but as there are straight joints, and no bonds where they meet the older walls, it would appear that neither of them was carried up simultaneously with the original building. On the east side of this cross wall the earth has been raised as much as six feet six inches above the set-off of the foundation, burying the old herringbone work, and rising nearly to the sills of the windows. This cross-wall—the lower part of which is rudely constructed, and is manifestly older than the superstructure—seems to have been placed here partly for the purpose of supporting the earth heaped up in forming the eastern platform, and partly, perhaps, to check the advance of the enemy, in case of the outer works of this part of the castle falling into his hands. There are no positive indications of any junction of the exterior walls with any other building, and it would seem, therefore, from the above description, that we have here the remains of a single isolated building, forming one long, narrow apartment of some kind, measuring internally about seventy-one feet by sixteen feet eleven inches.

One remarkable feature of this building is that the set-off of the foundation slopes upwards about six feet seven inches from west to east, and the floor of the apartment, therefore, no doubt, followed the same inclination. But the slope is not continuous in the same plane throughout, as west of the cross wall it is very slight, whilst at the spot where that wall now stands there seems to have been a sudden rise of about two feet nine inches. Here, therefore, there may possibly have been steps. The windows, in a great measure, corresponded with the slope of the floor, as they rise in the same direction about nine inches, one above the other. No pavement has been met with, but the ground seems to have been covered with mortar, in which a pavement might have been originally laid.

Near the west end of the existing herringbone wall, at about three feet six inches above the bottom of the foundation, is what looks much like a drain, neatly constructed of ashlar. It does not penetrate beyond the herringbone wall, and runs

in a somewhat diagonal direction. It is evidently an insertion of more recent date than the wall itself, but what purpose it was intended to serve is difficult to decide. It is shown in the accompanying wood-cut, which represents the western portion of the herringbone wall as far as the cross wall. The original window on the left of the engraving is partly ruined, but sufficient of it remains to show that it was identical in form and size with the others, which are perfect. The artist, therefore, has transferred one of the latter to this place in the engraving.

Some portion of the herringbone work is concealed by plaster of late date, as is shown in the accompanying view.

For what purpose was this building erected? To what use was it appropriated? The question is one which the evidence hardly warrants our answering with absolute certainty, and we are therefore driven to conjecture. On the whole, however, I am inclined to think it was a church. Could it have been the same which was built by the great St. Aldhelm, then abbot of Malmesbury, but afterwards bishop of Sherborne, in the last decade of the 7th century? If such was really the case this time-worn fragment and this hallowed spot cannot fail to awaken the most lively interest.

The question is considered more in detail, and some account of a church built by St. Aldhelm is given in the appendix at the end of the volume, to which the reader should refer.

A little westward of the herringbone wall there is a low pointed arch without mouldings, springing from plain chamfered imposts. It is not carried through the wall, and is too low for a doorway from the present level of the ground, so that its purpose is not easily determined.

Further on, and standing on the extreme western spur of the hill, are the remains of an octagon tower, which, from its position, obtained the name of the "Butavant"—the *bout-avant*, or prominent point. It seems to have had three stories: the lowest was beneath the level of the area of the ward, and was probably used as an *oubliette* approached through an opening in the floor above, for it had no apertures in the walls for admission of light. Treswell's plan describes this tower as "the dungeon," indicating that it was used as a prison, though the name "dungeon" was more properly descriptive of the keep, and as such it is generally used in France. The ground floor is on a level with the court-yard, and on the south side of it the remains of a loop are visible. This loop, however, does not seem to have raked the adjoining curtain. It rather looks as if the curtain was built subsequently to the tower in such a position as partially to obstruct the loop. But little of the tower now remains, and that little has been wholly robbed of its outer face, leaving us in ignorance whether it was cased with ashlar or only with hammer-dressed stone. A newel stair in the thickness of the wall led up to its upper apartments. More of the walls was recently standing, but a violent gale of wind on 11th Feb., 1866, following heavy rain which had disintegrated the masonry, blew down a large portion of it into the stream which flows at the base of the hill.

Adjoining this tower was a gardrobe, the vault of which remains. A stone projecting from the wall above served to carry the cross timber or ridge piece, to which a lean-to roof was framed. It has been fancifully described as a gallows! Below are portions of a jamb and head of a low doorway which led to this apartment.

Between this tower and the next, towards the east, a postern doorway is indicated in Treswell's plan, but the masonry, which has been disturbed, no longer exhibits traces of any such having existed.

The tower facing the north in this ward, which Hutchins calls the "prison chapel," though on what authority he does not say, was originally built with three loops, like the other mural towers of the castle. It is evident, therefore, that it could not have been originally intended for a chapel, and its dimensions are too small for it to have been so used. The loops have been blocked up and replaced in comparatively modern times, by three rectangular openings for windows. Weather mouldings, and a hole for a beam to rest in, seem to show that at some time or other there was a high pitched roof, which did not rise above the walls of the tower. What looks like a spout outside, seems to show that there was a central gutter. A modern fire-place has been inserted in the eastern wall. Treswell's drawing shows that in his time the gorge of the tower was closed by a wall with a door and window. At that time, therefore, it had probably been rendered habitable.

Some modern arches and stone benches for seats have been inserted in the walls of this ward, which was probably done in the 17th century, though tradition has assigned them to Sir Thomas I'Anson, sometime rector of the parish.

THE THIRD AND FOURTH WARDS, OR OLD BAILEY.

A steep and narrow ascent from the north-east angle of the second ward, having the curtain wall on the left, and the high bank which supports "the new bulwark" on the right, leads up to the site of the third gate, which opened into a small area called the third ward. Immediately opposite this was the fourth gate of the castle, opening to the fourth ward. Here we enter on the castle proper, occupying the highest of the three platforms, which form the surface of the castle hill. In this were the principal dwellings of the fortress, the first two wards being merely in the nature of outworks, though each was capable of separate defence. The two last gateways are utterly destroyed, and even their exact sites cannot now be distinguished. Neither of them appears to have been protected by a gatehouse—at least none such appears in Treswell's plan.

After passing the site of the third gate, we enter on a scene of chaos and confusion which baffles all description. Here the utter destruction of the buildings is the most apparent, and the effect of the enormous force of gunpowder cannot fail to excite astonishment as well as regret. Heaps of rubbish now overgrown with weeds and nettles, and immense masses of masonry, once forming part of the noble dungeon tower or keep, but still holding together like great fragments of rock, lie scattered around in the utmost confusion. The greater part of the other buildings which stood on this platform have also been thrown down, so that it is impossible, even with the assistance of Treswell's plan, drawn when the castle was perfect, to make out with anything like certainty what was their original arrangement.

The dungeon, or keep, which Treswell calls the king's tower, represented in the engraving opposite, stands proudly above the rest of the fortress, and occupies the highest point of the hill at the south-west corner of the upper platform. It rises immediately from the brink of the steep grassy chalk cliff, which separates this ward from the outer bailey, the southern wall being carried some way down the face of the acclivity. It was rectangular in form, and nearly square, like most other early Norman dungeons, and it nearly ranges with the cardinal points of the compass, though its southern face inclines a little towards the west. Only its south side and small portions of the east and west walls still remain standing. The rest has been so utterly overthrown that the whole of the foundations cannot

CORFE CASTLE.

The Keep or Dungeon Tower, from the South.

CORFE CASTLE.

castle ward. Here we enter on the castle proper, occupying the highest of the three platforms, which form the surface of the castle hill. In this were the principal buildings of the fortress, the first two wards being merely in the nature of outworks, though each was capable of separate defence. The two last gateways are utterly destroyed, and even their exact sites cannot now be distinguished. Neither of them appears to have been protected by a gatehouse—at least none with appears in Treswell's plan.

After passing the site of the third gate, we enter on a scene of chaos and confusion which baffles all description. Here the utter destruction of the buildings is the most apparent, and the effect of the enormous force of gunpowder cannot fail to excite astonishment as well as regret. Heaps of rubbish now overgrown with weeds and nettles, and immense masses of masonry, once forming part of the noble dungeon tower or keep, but still holding together like great fragments of rock, lie scattered around in the utmost confusion. The greater part of the other buildings which stood on this platform have also been thrown down, so that it is impossible, even with the assistance of Treswell's plan, drawn when the castle was perfect, to make out with anything like certainty what was their original arrangement.

The dungeon, or keep, which Treswell calls the king's tower, represented in the engraving opposite, stands proudly above the rest of the fortress, and occupies the highest point of the hill at the south-west corner of the upper platform. It rises immediately from the brink of the steep grassy chalk cliff, which separates this ward from the outer bailey, the southern wall being carried some way down the face of the archway. It was rectangular in form, and nearly square, like were the early Norman dungeons, and is nearly square with the cardinal points of the compass, though its southern face inclines a little towards the west. Only its south side and small portions of the east and west walls still remain standing, but it has been so utterly overthrown that the whole of its foundations can

CORFE CASTLE

The Keep or Dungeon Tower from the South.

now be clearly traced. Abutting against its western side was a staircase turret now almost entirely destroyed, but on the southern side a projecting turret or annexe has escaped destruction.

The eastern wall of the keep exhibits a remarkable example both of the extraordinary strength of Norman masonry and of the partial—it may almost be called the capricious—operation of explosive power. The north and south ends of the wall have been wholly destroyed, leaving the central portion— a mere strip—standing uninjured, and apparently unshaken. This fragment is now unfortunately wholly obscured by ivy, but if it could be examined it would present some interesting features.

According to Treswell's ground plan,* the keep stood apart and unconnected with the other dwellings, so that in fact it may have formed a distinct and separate fortress. But the bird's-eye view* (which, however, cannot be relied on for accuracy) seems to indicate that there was no interval between the keep and the adjacent buildings on the east.

The old plan of the ground floor [see plan A, page 68] shows a doorway near the north end of the east wall, which may have led into some adjoining building, though posterns are rare in Norman keeps. But it is equally possible that it might have merely given access to a mural stair, such as, there can be little doubt, was the case with the door indicated near the south-east corner of the first floor, in plan B. But if there was any building abutting against the east side of the keep, it must have been of limited width, for otherwise it would have blocked up a window in the great hall. Neither could it have been carried higher than the ground floor, as is evident from the positions of the windows in the apartments above.

The southern exterior has four flat buttresses of three stages, running almost to the summit, each being five feet seven inches wide, and projecting from the walls one foot four and a-half inches at the base. The upper stages of these buttresses

* See it at the end of the volume.

68   CORFE CASTLE.

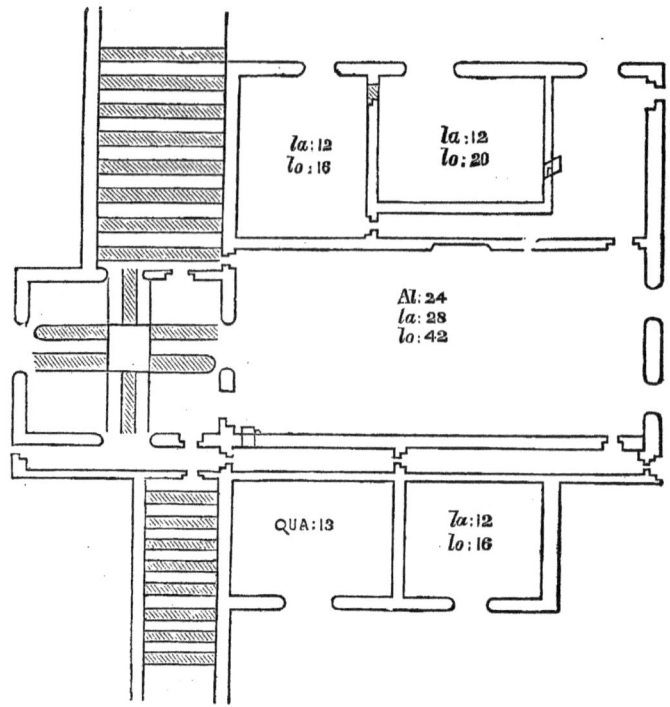

[Plan A.—Old Plan of ground floor of Great Tower, reduced from original.*]

recede very slightly from the faces of those immediately below them, but the set-offs are so slight that they may easily escape observation. The buttresses are twelve feet apart. On the west side they were five in number.

The walls at the basement, which have the spreading plinth, common in Norman buildings, are about seven feet thick; those of the floor above rather less, and there is a very slight set-off running round the outside of the whole of so much of the building as remains where the second floor commences. From this point upwards a close examination may possibly detect some little difference in the masonry or material, as if it was built at a somewhat later period than the rest. The walls were never carried higher than they are now seen, as a small fragment of the battlement very lately remained.

See remarks in the Introduction.

The masonry consists of well-cut ashlar, both within and without. Its stones are generally nearly square, and the joints are sometimes nearly an inch in width. All these features are characteristic of early Norman work.

The tower measures internally, on the basement floor or "vaults," as Treswell incorrectly calls them, thirty-nine feet three inches from east to west, but forty-three feet six inches on the ground floor immediately above, where the walls are not so thick. It was wider from north to south, but its dimension in that direction cannot now be accurately made out, though it seems to have been about fifty feet.

A strong party-wall, as was usual in Norman dungeons, divided the keep into two parts. In this instance it ran from east to west. There are no remains of mural passages, or any indications of a well such as are usually found in Norman buildings of this character. The joist holes of the large and massive timbers which supported the several floors are conspicuous in the interior of the wall still standing.

Great alterations have been made, from time to time, in the arrangement of all this part of the castle, and the walls have been much cut about. None of the original windows remain, with the exception hereafter mentioned, but several square-headed ones, and a doorway with a low four-centred arch have been inserted, either in the time of Henry VII., or by Sir Christopher Hatton, in the 16th century. An external arcade appears to have run round the whole of the upper story. Semicircular arches, mostly in pairs, springing from square imposts and jambs, occupy the spaces between the buttresses. These arches seem to have been merely ornamental, for there is no appearance in the masonry of their ever having been carried through the wall, neither can any traces of windows in connection with them be discovered in the inside. A pair of these arches in the isolated fragment of the eastern wall, now unfortunately entirely hidden by ivy, were visible within my recollection. The arcade is very similar in character to that seen in the White Tower of London, but more complete.

Underneath the whole of the keep were what Treswell designates "vaults," though they were separated from the apartments above them by a floor of timber. They are now nearly filled up with rubbish. At the south-east corner there is an arch incised in the face of the wall, and there seems to have been at this spot some stone vaulting, a springer of which remains. Possibly it may have supported a stair leading up to the doorway immediately above.

The ground floor [plan A] surmounting the basement or "vaults," was approached by what may be termed the grand staircase, carried up against the outside of the western face of the keep, and supported by a wide semicircular groined arch, the imposts and springer of which remain, though the stairs are utterly gone. Underneath this arch was an entrance to the basement, but it was not original. On the summit of the external stairs a large semicircular headed doorway, still perfect, led into the stair turret above mentioned, built outside of, and abutting against, the western face of the keep. This staircase turret was only carried to the height of the first floor. The stairs were arranged in short flights of steps, probably of timber, alternating with landings, carried round a small square central block, the whole occupying an area measuring internally sixteen feet five inches square. On the north side of this staircase is a fragment of an original Norman window. A wide semicircular headed doorway led from the staircase into a spacious and lofty apartment on the ground floor, which, according to the old plan, was twenty-four feet high and forty-two feet long by twenty-eight feet wide. It was lighted by two windows at its east end, and another looking on the external stairs toward the west, vestiges of all which are still distinguishable.

This floor had three other rooms, and a passage on the north side of the party-wall above mentioned, now wholly destroyed.

DESCRIPTION. 71

Above this, the first floor [see plan B] was entered from the top of the stairs* by a spacious doorway surmounted by a semi-circular arch, springing from imposts slightly ornamental, one of

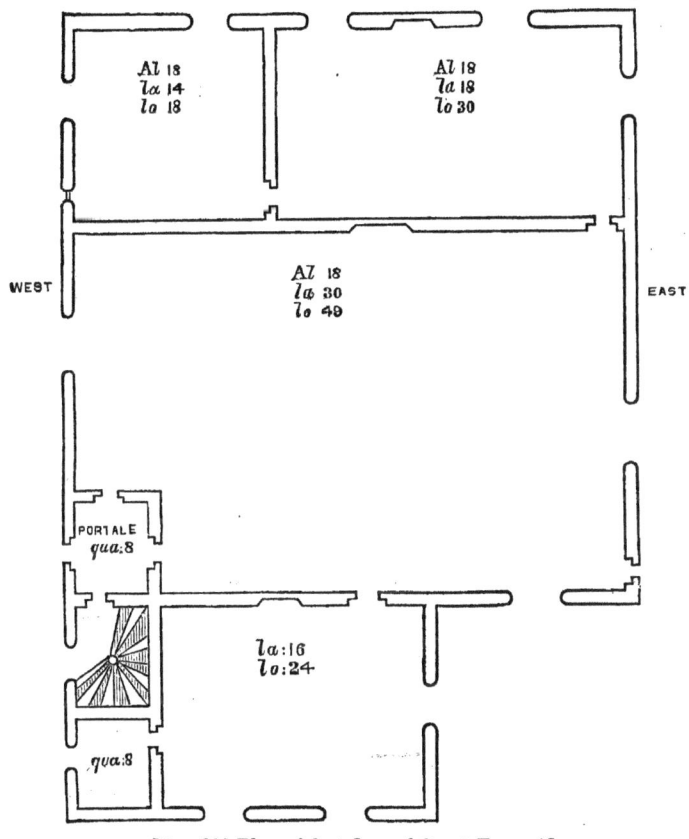

WEST

Al 18
la 14
lo 18

Al 18
la 18
lo 30

Al 18
la 30
lo 49

PORTALE
qua:8

la:16
lo:24

qva:8

EAST

[B.—Old Plan of first floor of Great Tower.†]

which still remains. This doorway was partially filled up, probably in the 16th century, when the smaller door, having a low four-centered arch, which still remains, was inserted. On this floor was another spacious room immediately over the one before described, and stated in the old plan to have been eighteen feet high and forty-nine feet long by thirty feet wide. These dimensions are not easily reconcilable with those of the

* The stairs are not shewn in the original Plan.
† See remarks in Introduction.

room underneath, as figured in the plan, or with the ruins, as they now exist; but the discrepancy may in some measure be accounted for by the walls being thinner in their upper stages than they are below, and perhaps we ought not to expect measurements to have been as carefully made in the time of Queen Elizabeth as they would be now. Adjoining the last-named apartment, and on the other side of the party-wall, were two other rooms, one being thirty feet by eighteen, and the other eighteen feet by fourteen.

There seems to have been originally only one story in the keep, above the ground floor. It was surmounted by a high pitched ridge and valley roof of two bays, which did not rise above the external walls. This is apparent from the weather mouldings still visible on the south wall, against which the roof abutted. A third story was subsequently constructed by substituting for the ridge and valley roof, a lead flat nearly on a level with the summit of the original roof. A design for the re-arrangement of apartments in this floor seems to be intended to be shown in plan C [page 73]; but it never could have been completely carried out: for the windows necessary for lighting the rooms, as they are delineated in the plan, were never made. Only one now exists, and there are no traces that there have at any time been more, as the masonry does not appear to have been disturbed. The plan, therefore, was probably only a design for contemplated improvements. That the roof, however, was at some time raised, and a third story was constructed, is apparent from the position of the fire-place and the one window which still remain. A small narrow window placed high up within the compass of the original high pitched roof is probably of early date.

A newel stair in the thickness of the wall, at the south-east corner, led from the first floor to the upper story and the battlements.

After the keep had been built, the wing or turret above mentioned was annexed to it on the south side, the architecture of which is in accordance with that of the building to which it adjoins; but straight joints in the masonry, and the absence of bond-stones, prove that it was

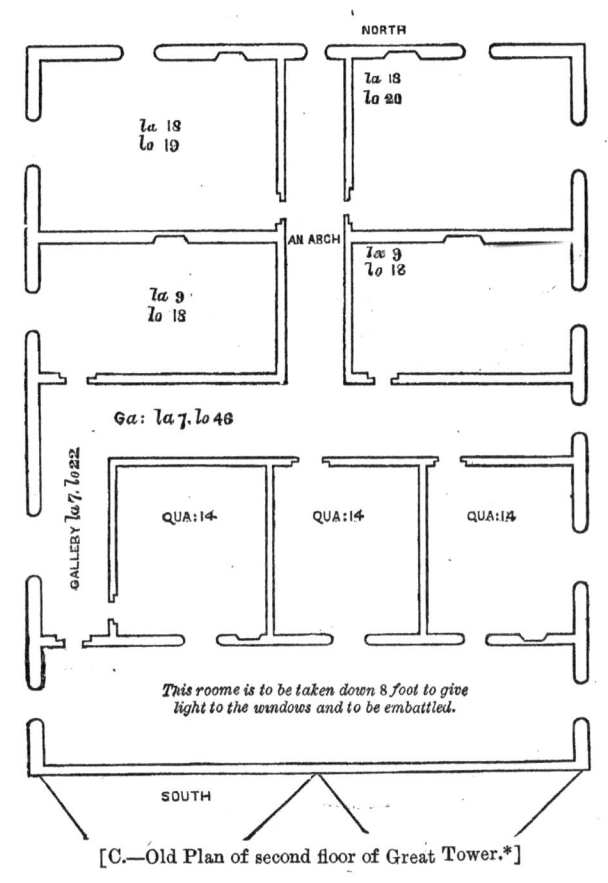

NORTH

la 18
lo 19

la 18
lo 20

AN ARCH

la 9
lo 18

la 9
lo 18

Ga: la 7. lo 46

GALLERY la 7. lo 22

QUA: 14

QUA: 14

QUA: 14

This roome is to be taken down 8 foot to give light to the windows and to be embattled.

SOUTH

[C.—Old Plan of second floor of Great Tower.*]

not carried up at the same time as the main building. It would almost seem, however, as if it had formed part of the original design of the great tower, though not simultaneously constructed, for no evidence has been detected in the masonry of there ever having been windows in the main building, where the addition abuts against it, or of the existing doorways being after-insertions. This annexe, as perhaps it may be called, contains on the ground floor two small

---

* See remarks in Introduction.

rooms, the western one measuring eight feet ten inches from east to west by seven feet three inches from north to south, the other nine feet three inches from east to west by seven feet three inches from north to south. They are separated from the main building by a gallery or passage, vaulted with stone, which is six feet wide between the buttresses, and twenty-eight feet eleven inches long to the outside of the walls. These dimensions cannot be reconciled with those given in the old plan, and the difference cannot be explained.

One of these rooms, the western one, was most probably a gardrobe and may have been one of the "gardrobes in the high tower," mentioned in the 19th Ed. II. The other apartment is wholly open to the gallery, the opening being spanned by a wide semicircular arch. In this room has been preserved the only original window in the keep. It looks towards the east, is square-headed on the outside, but its internal splay is surmounted by a round-headed arch. It may be distinguished in the wood-cut, facing page 66, where it forms little more than a square speck. In both the apartments, just described, larger square-headed windows, placed high above the floor have been inserted, probably in the 16th century, but traces of some of the original windows remain. There are indications of wooden floors to both these apartments on a level with the adjoining gallery, but it is uncertain what was below them, probably—at least as regards one of them—only the vault of the gardrobe, but the space is now filled with earth and rubbish. In the east and west walls of the largest of these apartments there are holes left in the masonry which, from their form, are unsuited for the support of joists, they look more as if they had been intended to receive the springers of ribs of a stone vaulting.

The mouths of two drains are apparent low down on the outside, no doubt connected with the gardrobes.

The gallery has lofty arched doorways at each end, which seem to have been originally intended to be left open, probably for the sake of ventilation of the gardrobes. There are now door jambs at the western opening, but they appear to be insertions. In the centre of this gallery, the masonry seems to indicate that other stone door jambs, not rising very high above the floor, have been inserted, after the original work was completed, which agrees with the old ground plan. But they have been subsequently cut away.

Two rounded-headed doorways lead from the grand apartment, above described, into this part of the great tower, the western one communicating directly with the gallery; the eastern one, by a short flight of steps in the thickness of the wall, giving access to the stairs by which the gallery was entered from the east.

Extending over both the rooms just described, as well as over the vaulted gallery, there was a single apartment measuring sixteen feet eight inches from north to south, by twenty-two feet ten inches from east to west on the floor level, but the roof was carried on about two feet farther west, and it covered also a narrow flight of stone steps, which appear to have led up to the parapet. These steps abut against the west wall, or rather they seem to have been constructed within its thickness. They were only two feet wide, and had no parapet. The floor of the apartment is on a somewhat higher level than that of the adjoining great hall, and the steps, commencing in the hall, were continued uninterruptedly through a large and lofty round-headed portal, which is made wide enough to serve also for an entrance into the apartment. A buttress, which would have inconveniently encroached on the width of the room, has been cut away or omitted from the floor level to the roof, above which it re-appears. The absence of bonding stones is even more conspicuous here than on the ground floor.

About four feet six inches from the east end is another door-way of smaller dimensions than the portal just described. It is square-headed, measuring in the opening seven feet three inches by three feet one inch, but it is surmounted by a semicircular arch. On the side next the great hall both doorways are perfectly plain, but the smaller one is handsomely ornamented within the apartment, the character of the ornaments being apparently of somewhat later date than that of the adjoining keep. Slender shafts set in an angle support imposts having a kind of volutes—as perhaps they may be called, and other simple ornaments springing from a ring of cable moulding, and supporting a square abacus. A plain roll moulding set in a hollow and surmounted by other simple members, runs round the arch. The tympanum is quite plain. Although this doorway has but one series of ornaments, and is somewhat more simple, its ornamentation is much of the same character as an example in the west end of Lincoln Cathedral, supposed to have been erected about 1090, and represented in the "Glossary of Architecture," 5th edition, vol. ii., plate 14; but the flat faces of the abacus are incised with an ornament very similar to one on the impost of a column in the Tower of London.*

There being an entire absence of ornamental work throughout the whole of the rest of the keep, it is in the highest degree improbable that this apartment would have been thus decorated if it had been a simple dwelling room. I make no doubt, therefore, that here we have what was called "the Chapel of St. Mary in the Tower of Corfe," and that this ornamented doorway was intended for the use of the priest. But besides this doorway we have still stronger evidence that this was a chapel, for there is an almery or locker in the wall not very high above the ground, on the north side of the place where the altar may have stood. It is quite plain and nearly square, measuring two feet two and a-half inches high by one foot ten inches wide. On the south side of the supposed site of the altar there is a hole in the wall near the ground, which may possibly have been connected with the drain of the piscina.

This chapel, if I may call it so, must have been rather low, but traces in the wall for lead flashings show that the

---

* See Glossary of Architecture, 5th edition, vol. ii., plate 45, No. 1.

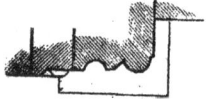

DOORWAY (RESTORED)

In the supposed "Chapel of St. Mary in the Tower of Corfe."

both doorways are perfectly plain, but the smaller one is handsomely ornamented within the apartment, the character of the ornaments being apparently of somewhat later date than that of the adjoining keep. Slender shafts set in an angle support imposts having a kind of volutes—as perhaps they may be called, and other simple ornaments springing from a ring of cable moulding, and supporting a square abacus. A plain roll moulding set in a hollow and surmounted by other simple members, runs round the arch. The tympanum is quite plain. Although this doorway has but one series of ornaments, and is somewhat more simple, its ornamentation is much of the same character as an example in the west end of Lincoln Cathedral, supposed to have been erected about 1088, and represented in the "Glossary of Architecture," 5th edition, vol. ii., plate 14; but the flat faces of the abacus are incised with an ornament very similar to one on the impost of a column in the Tower of London.*

There being an entire absence of ornamental work throughout the whole of the rest of the keep, it is in the highest degree improbable that this apartment would have been thus decorated if it had been a simple dwelling room. I make no doubt, therefore, that here we have what was called "the Chapel of St. Mary in the Tower of Corfe," and that this ornamental doorway was intended for the use of the priest. But besides this doorway we have still stronger evidence that this was a chapel, for there is an almery or locker in the east wall, some height above the ground, on the north side of the place where the altar may have stood. It is quite plain and nearly square, measuring two feet two and a-half inches high by one foot ten inches wide. On the south side of the supposed site of the altar there is a hole in the wall near the ground, which may possibly have been connected with the drain of the piscina.

This chapel, if I may call it so, must have been rather low, but traces in the wall for lead flashings show that the

* See Glossary of Architecture, 5th edition, vol. ii., plate 45, No. 1.

DOORWAY (RESTORED)

In the supposed "Chapel of St Mary in the Tower of Corfe."

To face page 76.

roof has been varied at different times, and that it was at one time, if not always, covered by a ridge and valley roof of two bays. This is shown in the old ground plan B, which also states that it was proposed to lower the room eight feet to give light to the adjoining rooms, and to embattle it. This may, perhaps, relate chiefly to the ridge and valley roof, which might have been intended to be replaced by a lead flat.

None of the original windows remain. Two square-headed ones on the south side, and one on the east, all deprived of their mullions, were inserted in the 16th century.*

As regards the date of the annexe relatively to that of the main building, perhaps there is some significance in the fact that both sides of the doorway above mentioned are not ornamented, as it seems likely they would have been if the two had been contemporaneously constructed.

Plan B is evidently intended to represent the upper floor of the annexe, but it is inaccurate, both in arrangement and dimensions, and the fire-place shown in it was never constructed. This was probably only a design for contemplated alterations, which were never entirely carried out.

Westward of the great tower, and extending beyond what was once the staircase turret, a narrow spur of the chalk hill abuts into the middle ward. On the summit of this, and on a level with the ground floor of the tower, was a small platform, artificially constructed, which Treswell's plan designates "the new bulwark." It had probably been adapted in modern times for the purpose of carrying the small pieces of ordnance which were mounted on it in the 16th century, and hence it acquired the above name. Part of a wall which supports it on the north side was carefully executed,

* It had always been a great puzzle to myself and others where to place this chapel of St. Mary, of which frequent mention is made, but of which no vestiges are met with elsewhere. The ornamental doorway above described is invisible from below, and the apartment is inaccessible except by the aid of a long ladder, by mounting which I have been enabled to examine it. It is not improbable that it may never before have been visited since the destruction of the castle, except occasionally by some adventurous boy who has contrived, I know not how, to climb up to it in search of birds' eggs. Its existence was unknown even to tradition.

and had several buttresses, now taken away; but the rest of the masonry on this side, as well as that on the west, is for the most part of very rude and clumsy construction. On the south side the whole of the masonry is gone. Access to "the new bulwark" was gained from the west end of the vaulted gallery, on the surface of a mass of masonry built up for the purpose against the south side of the staircase turret, and which appears, on close examination, to have been constructed prior to the erection of the curtain wall, on the summit of which was a narrow flight of steps leading down from the west end of the gallery to the second gateway. The whole of this mass, having been undermined (for it seems to have been used as a stone quarry), fell away bodily a few years ago, and part of it, lodging near the second gateway, partially blocked up the road, whilst the rest, continuing its headlong course, rolled down into the stream below.

The southern side of the annexe has been undermined with a view to its destruction, but though the wall remains without support, so hard and adhesive is the mortar, and so strong is the masonry, that it still hangs together as firmly as if supported by an arch. The eastern corner has been recently underpinned but the precaution was unnecessary, as there is no sign that any settlement had occurred.

The annexe did not cover more than about two-thirds of the width of the keep, and abutting against the portion of the wall not so covered a staircase was constructed, leading down from the gallery to the court-yard below. It was enclosed by a wall on the opposite side, and was covered by a lean-to roof, a chace of which is visible in the main wall, and shown in the wood-cut.

Descending these stairs we enter what was once a small court-yard. It was, perhaps, a back court or kitchen court, as the kitchen was at its north-east corner. The kitchen has been utterly destroyed, and even its materials must have been carted away, though faint traces seem to remain of the ovens indicated in the plan.

Separated from this court by a wall on the east side was another court, and both these courts, being surrounded on the other sides by the apartments of the castle, were enclosed on the south by a wall of very rude masonry, crowning the precipice which intervenes between the outer and inner wards. An opening has been made in the centre of this wall to give access to a small bastion for cannon, which, as it is unnoticed by Treswell, was probably constructed during the civil wars.

On the east and south of the second court-yard, just described, rose a mass of building which Treswell designates "the Queen's Tower." It was built on vaults, not, however, sunk below the natural level of the ground, and contained several apartments which are now wholly destroyed, with the exception of the great hall and its approaches, parts of which remain.

A short flight of steps near the north-east corner of the kitchen led to a vestibule, about twenty feet by ten feet, now partly destroyed. There were apartments over both the stairs and vestibule. Traces of the stairs by which they were reached still remain. In the first-mentioned staircase are two small square-headed windows, nine inches wide by three feet six inches high, looking towards the south, and in the vestibule are remains of a lancet window towards the north. The east wall of the vestibule immediately opposite the head of the stairs, is faced with ashlar, and had two large handsome pointed doorways, side by side, exactly similar, and excellent in design and execution. One of them is almost perfect, but of the other only one jamb remains. The one on the right led into the great hall, which stands in the direction of north and south. It was forty-six feet long by twenty-three feet wide, and had three pointed windows looking towards the east, and two on the opposite side. The south end had none, and the north end is wholly destroyed. Part of the eastern wall of this hall is tolerably perfect. The windows have stone seats or benches on each side, within the splays, which proves that this apartment was a hall, and not, as some have imagined, a chapel.* The eastern exterior is handsomely built of ashlar, and has two buttresses of two stages, as well as good label mouldings over the windows. No tracery remains in the windows, though they probably originally consisted of two lights. The walls were never much higher than at present, for part of the corbel table which supported the parapet or spring of the roof is still to be seen. The other doorway, before mentioned, which adjoins the one leading into the hall, led to an apartment of which only the smallest fragment now remains. It adjoined the north end of the hall, and judging from the foundation, and some fragments of wall which still survive, it could have been little more than eleven or twelve feet wide. Its length corresponded with the width of the hall. It seems to have been vaulted and groined with stone, a portion of a springer of the groining being still visible in the angle just within the doorway. The springer was supported by a slender shaft of Purbeck marble, set in a hollow, on either side of which was another hollow, having a roll moulding within it. The purpose to which this small apartment was appropriated can only be a matter of conjecture. The very little of it which remains is of an ecclesiastical character, and I think it was probably a small chapel or oratory for the private use of the royal family, or chief inmates of the castle, though its dimensions seem to have been almost too small even for this.

In the 14th Ed. III., the chapel of the "Gloriet" is mentioned, and if that chapel was not here, it is difficult to find a place for it elsewhere. The chapel, dedicated to St. Mary, is usually described as in the Tower.

That here was an apartment distinct from the hall is

---

* Had it not been for these window benches, this building might, in some respects, have accorded with the notices of "the chapel," or "the chapel of the Gloriet." But the benches are very characteristic. Besides which, if this had been a chapel, it would seem to have cut off communication between the kitchen and the tower of the Gloriet, with its adjacent dwelling rooms.

apparent, not only from the character of the ornamentation above-mentioned, but from its being approached through a doorway close to that of the adjacent hall, for the hall would not have required two doors side by side. The size and character of the second doorway, too, seems to indicate that it led to some apartment at least equally important with the hall.

The architecture of the hall, with its vestibule and adjacent apartment or chapel, is of early English character, and the building was probably erected late in the reign of King Henry III.

At the south-east angle of this part of the castle are remains of very massive walls, ten feet thick, which have been undermined and displaced like the walls of the other external towers. The natural strength of this spot must have rendered unnecessary so thick a wall, unless it was intended to carry a weighty superstructure. Here, therefore, was probably the tower called the tower of the "Gloriet," hereafter mentioned—a name which seems to have been sometimes given to the whole of the eastern portion of the castle. The same name is met with at Leeds Castle in Kent and it was most probably adopted here, as elsewhere, from the lofty spot on which the erection stood, and the extensive view which it commanded of the surrounding country. A building constructed on the most elevated spot of the grounds of the Imperial Palace at Schönbrunn, near Vienna, from whence an extensive view is obtained of the city and environs, is called "La Gloriette."

To the south of the hall just described, and adjoining the tower of the Gloriet, are some remains of vaulting, and over this, extending towards the west, and overhanging the outer ward, there seem to have been several other apartments which no longer exist. A gardrobe is indicatad in Treswell's plan, and some remains of it are discernible in the southern wall. On the east side of what I have conjectured to be the chapel of the Gloriet, a hollow in the ground shows the site of a well which must have been sunk before the adjoining building was erected: for according to Treswell's plan the wall was so adjusted as to accommodate it. The well must have been of great depth, being, no doubt, carried down below the base of the hill. It is at a spot nearest to the spring called St. Edward's fountain, which rises immediately below.

Adjoining the north-west corner of the kitchen was a flight of steps, apparently an external one, leading to the upper floors. To the north of the supposed chapel of the Gloriet, and occupying the north-east corner of the upper platform, was a small garden, separated by a wall from the fourth ward. At the north-east corner of that ward, and rising out of the outer wall, was a small square mural tower, of two stories above the basement, originally approached by a covered way from the passage leading to the hall. This may have been the tower called Cokayne, so named from its pleasant situation,* and the grand and extensive view which it commanded over the adjacent country. From its position it was admirably adapted for a watch tower.

A little to the west of this a fragment which has fallen from the great tower exhibits some herring-bone work, but it is manifestly the back of a fire-place, this kind of masonry continuing in use for the backs of fire-places long after it had ceased to be adopted in the construction of main walls.

* "*Pays de Cocagne,*" a plesant country to live in.

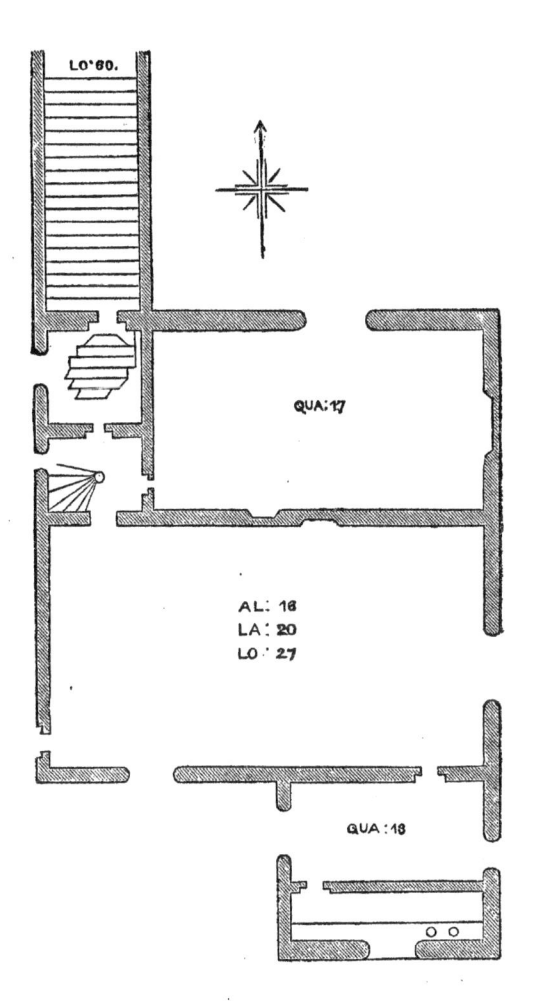

PLAN D.

Found at Kingston Lacey with plans A, B and C. It probably relates to some portion of Corfe Castle now destroyed.

THE FABRIC.

It would add greatly to the interest of Corfe Castle, if we could ascertain with certainty where all the different towers, courts, and apartments, the names of which have been recovered, were respectively situated, but so complete has been the destruction, so utter is the confusion, that the task seems entirely hopeless.

No doubt great changes have, from time to time, throughout a long series of years, been made in several parts of the castle, so that buildings, or apartments, which are mentioned at one time, may have ceased to exist, or have become known by other names at subsequent periods.

In contemporary accounts we have notices of the "hall," or dwelling in the ward, outside the Great Tower. This was in the time of King John. Later than this there were the King's Hall, the Long Hall, the Long Chamber, the King's Chamber, the King's Great Chamber, the Queen's Chamber, the Porch before the Queen's Chamber, the Chamber of the King and Queen, the Chamber called the "Gloriet," the Chamber next the Chapel, the Oriel before the King's Chapel, the Parlour, the Constabulary, the Wine Cellar, the Kitchen and the Bakery.

Of the towers, besides the Butavant, already noticed, there was "the Tower," and "the High Tower," which were, no doubt, the same; and the towers called Cockayne, Plente, Plenteye, or Plentethe, Swalewe, Malemit, and Sauvary, the two last, as well as the Butavant, being spoken of as prisons. Frequent mention is also made of "the Chapel." "The King's Chapel," "the Chapel of St. Mary," and "the Chapel of the 'Gloriet,'" are also repeatedly named.

The King's Hall and the Long Chamber were contiguous to each other, and the latter was near the tower, *juxta turrim*. The Long Chamber was also next the King's Chamber, so that perhaps the King's Chamber and the King's Hall may have been identical. The Long Hall was likewise near the King's Chamber, and was therefore probably the same as the Long Chamber. The King's Chamber (unless there was another so called) adjoined, or was near to *(juxta)* the kitchen in the "Gloriet," but the king's chambers in the "Gloriet" are mentioned in the plural.

An inquisition hereafter more particularly mentioned, taken in the 19th Ed. II., respecting the condition of the castle, seems to show that the King's Hall, the Chapel of St. Mary, the Long Hall, the Parlour, the "*Porchea ante cameram Reginæ*" and consequently, we may assume, the Queen's Chamber itself, were not within the four walls of the Great Tower; because the same return, while describing the state of the above-mentioned apartments, also reports, as a separate item, the condition of "the High Tower with its chambers and gardrobes"—"High Tower" being a name frequently used to designate the Great Tower, dungeon, or keep.

The "Gloriet" was certainly a part of the castle distinct from "the Tower;" and although, in 3rd Ric. II., "a tower called Gloriet," was built, and in 8th, 13th, 14th Ed. I.. the chamber called "La Gloriet" is mentioned, other notices seem to imply that the "Gloriet" contained more than one apartment. In 30th Ed. III., the king's chamber next the kitchen, in the "Gloriet" is frequently spoken of, and the "Gloriet" certainly contained a chapel. Perhaps the whole of the extreme eastern portion of the dwellings of the castle may have been known by this name, and have been thus distinguished from the great tower or keep. There were at least two chapels * within the castle: though "the chapel," without further description, is most frequently spoken of.

In 23rd Henry III., the king commanded the sheriff of the county to cause to be paid to each of two chaplains of his Castle of Corfe 50s. for their stipend, and a like sum to the chaplain ministering in the chapel of St. Aldhelm, near (*juxta*) Corfe, as well as 50s. to the king's chaplain ministering in the chapel of St. Edward, at Corfe,† which latter is now the parish church. But from 20th Hen. III. to 6th Ed. I., the sheriff, in his annual account of disbursements, only enters the payment of one, who is described as ministering in the chapel of St. Mary in the Tower, though he is always coupled with the chaplain ministering in the chapel of St. Aldhelm, in Purbeck.

In the 11th and 12th Ed. I., the chapel of St. Mary is described as in the upper dungeon. This shows that it was in an upper floor of the keep. In 19th Ed. II. it is spoken of as "within the 3rd gate;" whilst in the same document the High Tower and its chambers and gardrobes are named as something distinct. There seems scarcely room for a chapel in the small ward between the 2nd and 3rd gates shown in Treswell's plan, and indeed it is somewhat questionable whether, until comparatively recent times, the 3rd ward was enclosed.

In 11th and 12th Ed. I. a mason was employed in working stone for the stairs before (*ante*) the chapel of St. Mary, in the upper dungeon, and also in working stone and laying it down for steps of the stairs leading to the Tower. This shows that the two stairs were distinct. "The stairs towards the Tower" doubtless signified the grand external stairs leading up to the keep, and "the stairs before the

---

* In the palace of Gillingham, in this county, the King and Queen had each a separate chapel.   † Liberate Roll.

Chapel of St. Mary, in the upper dungeon" fits the description before given of what I suppose to have been that chapel. Wherever such chapel was situated, it was immediately under the roof, as appears by the accounts of the repairs.

If Treswell's bird's-eye-view is faithful, the Great Tower was joined on its eastern side by a block of buildings which rose nearly as high as the tower itself, and extended almost to the eastern curtain wall. This would embrace what he calls the Queen's Tower, and the apartment which he designates the kitchen. But here we are met by a difficulty, because the Fabric Rolls show that in the 8th Ed. I., two coverers (tilers) were paid for repairing the kitchen, and in 32nd Ed. III., two men were paid for taking down the old kitchen; stone was provided for supporting the wall *(ad sustenendum murum)*, and tiles and crests were purchased for covering it. This looks as if there was nothing over it; but on the other hand a flight of steps occurs in Treswell's plan at one corner of the kitchen, which shows there must then have been apartments above it. Were there two kitchens?

Undoubtedly the oldest part of Corfe Castle is the fragment of herringbone work already described at page 63. Its antiquity has been considered under the "General Description," on page 59, and is further noticed in the appendix.

Queen Elfrida's residence here is spoken of by Malmesbury as her "villa;" and by Knighton as her "*hospitium;*" whilst the author of Brompton's Chronicle is more specific, for he says the murder of King Edward the Martyr was committed at Elfrida's "house" *(domus)* at Corph, adding "*ubi nunc castrum satis clebre constructum est,*" so that, according to his view, no castle properly so called existed here at that time. Polidore Virgil describes the Queen's residence as "*œdes Elfridœ,*" and adds, "*Est eo loco hodie arx quam apellant Corpham.*" With the exception of the fragment of wall just mentioned no part of the castle is ascertained to be older than the Norman Conquest.

The earliest notice we have of the spot is a gift by King Edred, great uncle of King Edward the Martyr, in the year 948, thirty-one years prior to the murder of the latter, to "a certain religious woman called Ælfthryth," supposed to have been second abbess of Shaftesbury, of seven manses in Purbeck, which by a subsequent charter of the same king, bearing date 956, are shown to have been at Corfe and Blachenwell. The genuineness of the Anglo-Saxon charters in the Shaftesbury cartulary, in which these grants are recorded.* is not well established; but that scarcely affects the question before us, for they are undoubtedly of great antiquity, and even forgers would be careful to describe correctly the property laid claim to. This is all that concerns us at present. The boundaries of the lands thus granted are set out in minute detail, many of the names made use of in the description still survive in a modified form, and their identification is of much importance, as will hereafter be shown, in helping us to ascertain the date at which the castle was first built. I have taken pains to trace these boundaries on the spot, and it is quite clear that they comprehend what afterwards constituted the manor of Kingston, *including the site of the now existing castle.*

The manor of Kingston was held, at the Domesday survey, by the then Abbess of Shaftesbury, but a most important foot-note is added to the description, stating that previous to the survey a portion of the manor, to the extent of one hide, had been given to the king by the abbess in exchange for the church of Gillingham, and that on this hide of land the king had built the Castle of Wareham. "*De manerio Chingeston habet Rex unam hidam in qua fecit Castellum Warham, et pro ea dedit Sanctæ Mariæ (Sceptesber), ecclesiam de Gillingham cum appendeciis suis.*" † The site of Wareham

---

* Harl. MS., No. 61. † Domesday.

Castle is not within the limits identified, as above-mentioned, with those of the manor of Kingston. It is nearly four miles distant from Corfe, and although, no doubt, outlying portions of land often in more recent times formed parcels of manors to which they were not contiguous, yet it is highly improbable that the site of the Castle of Wareham, which is well ascertained, should ever have belonged to a religious house. A hide of land would embrace a considerable portion of the town of Wareham, whereas the site of the castle and of its immediate precincts amounts to much less than this. Wareham is a place of great antiquity, and the castle was built on a spot within the circuit of its walls which is the most likely one to have been originally selected for the purpose. It is in the highest degree improbable that such a site would ever have come into possession of a nunnery, or have remained in such hands until Wareham had acquired the importance as a place of strength which it had reached before the Norman Conquest. We are compelled, therefore, to look for some explanation of this ambiguous passage, and though the evidence which can be adduced for its solution is indirect, yet it appears to me to be sufficiently conclusive.

The transaction mentioned in Domesday is repeated in the ancient document called the "Testa de Nevill," which says that the advowson of the church of Gillingham was given to St. Edward (*i.e.*, to the Abbey of Shaftesbury) in exchange for the land where the Castle of *Corf* is placed (*"advocatio ecclesie de Gillingeham, data fuit abb'i de S'co Edwardo in escambium, pro terra ubi Castellum de Corf positum est."*)* This is in direct contradiction to the words of Domesday, and one or other must be wrong. The "Testa de Nevill" is not an original document, but a compilation of the time of Edward I. from inquisitions taken in that and the preceding reigns, and its contents, though not having the legal authority of records, were considered as "evidences"

---

* Testa de Nevill.

by the Barons of the Exchequer. Now, if we can be content to assume that the evidence which satisfied the Barons of the Exchequer of old was sufficient, the difficulty is explained, and it was the place where the Castle of *Corfe*, not the Castle of Wareham, was built that was given by the Abbess of Shaftesbury to the King in exchange for the advowson of Gillingham, and this castle, we are told in Domesday, was built by the Conqueror himself, "*ubi fecit castellum,*" &c.

But how is this direct contradiction in terms to be reconciled? It may be done by supposing that the commissioners who made the returns from which Domesday was compiled, or the Normans who were employed to transcribe and arrange them, inadvertently wrote Wareham for Corfe; or more probably the castle was considered as a kind of outpost of the then important town of Wareham—in fact, the Castle of Wareham at Corfe—and they therefore gave to it the name of the town. An instance of the name of one place being used by chroniclers in the 12th century indiscriminately for that of another, there being a feudal connection between the two, is mentioned by Mr. Freeman in his Life of William Rufus. Tickhill, in Yorkshire, he says, not uncommonly took the name of Blyth, in Nottinghamshire, the two places being about three miles distant from each other.

That the passage in Domesday relates to Corfe and not to Wareham is supported by indirect documentary evidence which is irreconcilable with the language of the Norman record, except on this hypothesis. Corfe in Purbeck is not mentioned in Domesday;* but no argument against the existence of a castle here can thence be deduced, for several castles are left unnoticed in the Great Record in the description of lands on which they stood. They are only incidentally

---

* A place named Corfe is mentioned in Domesday amongst the possessions of Robert Fitz Girold, but its identity with Corfe Mullen, near Wimborne, is satisfactorily proved by its feudal dependance on the manor of East Camel, in Somersetshire, which passed, together with Corfe Mullen, to William de Romara representative of Robert Fitz Girold.

named in other passages, and we are told that the Conqueror exceded all his ancestors in the number of the castles which he built.

That the site of Corfe Castle was parcel of the possessions of the Crown when Domesday was compiled is proved by a record of 2nd Ric. II.,* wherein the Castle of Corfe is stated to be "ancient demesne of the Crown." Now, this tenure could only attach to land which belonged to the Crown at the compilation of Domesday—Domesday Book itself being the test which was appealed to for proof of the existence of such tenure in any particular case. No lands, in fact, but those which were held by the King in demesne at the great survey were considered to be "*de antiquo dominico coronæ.*" The verdict thus shows that in the opinion of the jury on the evidence produced on this occasion, the site of Corfe Castle was the property of the Crown when Domesday was compiled.

There is further evidence in Domesday which, when explained by subsequent events, helps to show that what is spoken of as Wareham Castle meant the Castle of Corfe. The manor of Moulham, in the parish of Swanage, comprising one hide of land, is described as the property of Durandus the Carpenter, one of the king's servants, and in after times it was held by a family who took the name of De Moulham, descendants, as is said, of Durandus, by the service of finding a carpenter to work about the Great Tower of Corfe Castle whenever it required repair, and the king put in his claim. That this service was imposed by the Conqueror himself when granting Moulham to his carpenter is more than probable, and it is most likely the grant was made in reward for the services which the master carpenter (or builder, as we should now designate him) had rendered in the construction of the castle. The duty to be performed is confined to the "Great Tower," and this is the part (if any) which, with the greatest probability, may be supposed to be the

* Pat., 2nd Rich. II, 2nd part. m. 13.

Conqueror's work. The rest, with the exception of the herringbone work before mentioned, is of later date.

There is an entry in the Pipe Roll of 31st H. I., forty-five years later than Domesday, which at first sight seems to countenance a literal interpretation of the last-mentioned record; but when carefully considered, it helps to confirm our theory. It says, "the carpenter of the Castle of Wareham" was excused the payment of 2s. for Danegeld. Now, it is pretty certain that this person, whoever he was, was no ordinary carpenter; for Danegeld was a land tax, and a mere carpenter earning daily wages would not in those days be possessed of land thus chargeable. The fact of his being described as "the carpenter" looks as if he held the land because he was of that trade, and because as such he had some special service to perform. The assessment of Danegeld was made on the inquest of Domesday, and the Barons of the Exchequer would expect the sheriff to account for the impost in accordance with the terms of that record. It would be immaterial to them to inquire what was the most correct name of the castle with which "the carpenter" was associated. There is no notice in Domesday of any other carpenter, except Durandus, who could be chargeable for the geld in Dorset. Neither is there any evidence that he or any other carpenter was charged with the repair of the castle in the town of Wareham. If, when the grant was made by the Conqueror, Corfe Castle was known as the Castle of Wareham at Corfe, Corfe might have been mentioned in the grant under the name of the Castle of Wareham. The fact of this carpenter being excused helps to identify him with Durandus, or his successor, for 2s. would be the tax payable for one hide of land, which was the quantity held by Durandus in Moleham. The carpenter, perhaps, had been inadvertently charged for this hide, and upon representing some legal exemption he had been excused. The *Inquisitio Gheldi* says that of half a hide (in Wilcheswood adjoining Moleham, which Durandus held of the wife of Hugh FitzGrip), the king took no geld, so that it is not improbable the carpenter was further favoured by having his lands exempted from the tax. But however this may be, the evidence above adduced seems to afford strong grounds for belief that the carpenter of Wareham Castle was no other than Durandus or his successor, and that in this instance also, what was termed Wareham Castle was in fact the castle at Corfe.

The keep, or great tower, was such a one as the Conqueror *may* have built; for though it presents many features which are characteristic of castles attributed to his immediate successors, we have no warrant for assuming that those features, which had become established in the time of the last-mentioned kings, were never adopted in buildings erected by the Conqueror himself at a period so little antecedent. The Bayeux tapestry shows that castles built of stone were not unknown to the architects of that day. There seems no warrant, therefore, for the supposition which has been advanced, that even if the Conqueror had built a castle here, it was of wood and not of stone.

In construction the keep of Corfe has many features in common with the White Tower in London, which is generally admitted to have been built by Bishop Gundulph before the close of the Conqueror's reign. If, therefore, there is no architectural peculiarity which is inconsistent with the supposition that the keep of Corfe was built by William the Conqueror, I see no valid reason for doubting that he was the founder.

It has already been stated (page 9) that a castle of some sort undoubtedly existed here within twenty years after the compilation of Domesday Book, as it was selected by King Henry I., in 1106, for the incarceration of his unfortunate brother, Robert Duke of Normandy. Twenty years after this, "*Corf Castellum juxta Warham*" is spoken of by William of Malmesbury in his "Gesta Pontificum," which has been supposed to have been written by him in 1125, 25th or 26th Hen. I.

In the time of King Stephen, Corfe (Corpha) is spoken of as one of the strongest castles in England.*

We next find it mentioned in the 8th year of King Hen. II., when the sheriff accounted for two shillings laid out on its repair † and it is again noticed in the Black Book of the Exchequer, compiled about 12th Hen. II., where it is stated that the free tenants of three knights fees, in the vill of Cerne, performed castle ward in the Castle of Corfe, when the king commanded their services.

In the following reign we have only notice of twenty shillings in the first year, one hundred shillings in the eighth, and twenty marks in the tenth year of King Richard I., laid out in repairs of the king's apartments in the castle, *domus*‡ *Regis in Castello de Corfi.*§

In the reign of King John, considerable sums were spent about the castle.

In the second year of this reign the sheriff of Dorset and Somerset accounts for 118*s.* 4*d.* laid out in the works of the castle, *(in operationibus Castelli di Corvo).* In the third year of that king he accounts at the exchequer for 100*s.* expended on the works of the Castle of Corfe; and in the following year £275 0*s.* 1*d.* were spent about the king's dwellings at Corfe, "*in operatione domorum Regis de Corf,*" and 20*s.* were spent in the repairs of the castle ; Robert de Clavell and William de Bosco being surveyors of the work. The same persons were surveyors 5th John, when the sum of £246 10*s.* 4*d.* was spent on the works of the castle, and also in the following year, when £127 6*s.* 4*d.* were laid out in the same way. The "custodes" of the *new work* at Corf had 140 marks. 7th John, 118*s.* 4*d.* were spent about the works, *Castelli di Corvo.*‖ 8th John, Geoffry Fitz Peter is ordered to pay out of the king's money

---

* Gesta Stephani. † Pipe Roll.
‡ The word "*domus*" continually occurs in these accounts and seems to signify something distinct from the fortifications of the castle. It may, perhaps, be properly rendered "dwellings," or apartments. The "*domus*" in the great tower are mentioned in 21st Ed. I. § Pipe Roll. ‖ *Ibid.*

to Stephen de Turnham and J. de Vipount £50 for work at the castle of Corf* 11th John, 75 marks of the issues of the Priory of Kenilworth, were paid by the hands of Master Henry de Cernell to Philip de Permenter, for works at the castle of Corfe.† 8th July, 15th John, the king commands William de Harecurt to allow for the works at Corf 300 marks out of the issues of the honor of Pontefract, which he had in his custody, and 15th Dec. following, the treasurer and chamberlains of the exchequer are commanded to deliver to William de Harecurt, by the hands of Richard Pippard, 80 marks for the works of the king's castle at Corfe.‡

10th July, 16th John, the king sent his thanks to the Bishop of Winchester for the diligence he had displayed in carrying on the works of the castle of Corfe, and commanded him to supply to William de Harcourt as much of the king's money as he should see fit for further executing the same.§

5th Sept. following, Constantine Brember is commanded to procure ships with all possible haste, and cause to be carried to Corfe the king's timber which was in his bailiwick, the cost to be accounted to him at the exchequer.‖

In the same year the king sends to William de Harecurt fifteen of his own miners and stonemasons *(minatores nostros et petrarios)*, to two of whom he had engaged to pay 6*d.* per diem, and to the rest 3*d.*, ordering that he should pay them the aforesaid wages from the 24th Nov., so long as they should be employed by him in working about the margin or bank of the foss at the Castle of Corfe *(in dova fossati apud castrum de Corf)*. The names of some of the workmen who were thus employed sound very foreign, and they were probably French—viz., Rob Angevin, Will de Bauc', Peter Bardin, Will Bonvis, Henri de Borchard, Will le Perier, Gerard de Vernon, Fulk de Bardevill, and Pet'r Pictav'. The king would hardly have sent to Corfe men of this kind,

* Close Roll. † Rot. de misis, &c., 11th John.
‡ Close Roll. § *Ibid.* ‖ *Ibid.*

who were usually in his own special employ, unless some works requiring more than ordinary care and skill—something, in short, different from a common bank, which local labourers could have easily raised—was at this time to be executed.

It is not easy to determine what was the precise nature of the work to be done, or at what spot. The term "*dova fossati*" means something different from the fosse itself, and in its primary sense would indicate a rampart or bank of earth thrown out from the fosse.* But "*dova*" may also mean the side or wall of a ditch or fosse,† such as the steep acclivity which rises from the present inner fosse of the castle to the base of the buildings on the upper platform, and which has evidently been artificially scarped. Except this, there is nothing connected with either fosse, as we now see them, which could have demanded any special engineering But the fosse alluded to could not have been the inner fosse in the shape in which it still exists, because at its eastern end it is sunk below the level of the foundations of the eastern wall, apparently built by King Henry III., so that the construction of the latter seems to be prior in point of date. Nevertheless, I am disposed to think that even in British and Roman periods, long before a castle of stone was built here, the hill was fortified by earthworks, and if so ditches would most likely have been dug very nearly on the sites of the existing fosses. The base of the gateway tower at the west end of the inner fosse stands about half way below its brink, and the fosse is carried on across the site of the western curtain wall, and some way down the face of the hill, where it gradually disappears. This continuation would hardly have been done after the castle, in its present state, had been built, and I suspect it is the

---

* A bank or rampart could not well have been thrown up on either margin of the outer fosse, because from the configuration of the ground it would have blocked up the entrance to the castle.

† "Nec dovis fossati,"—" Sur la dove d'un fosse,"—" Quibus ultimis locis intelligenda fossæ margo, seu terra ex fossato circumjecta."—Ducange.

remains of a very ancient earthwork, greatly modified in more recent times.

17th John, 50s. were spent in the repairs of the dwellings of the castle *(domorum in castro).**

Thus, during the reign of this king, we have notices of various sums, amounting in the aggregate to £1,006 12s. 5d., having been spent about the works of the castle, in repairs and new buildings, which proves that a great deal was done at this time.

In the time of King Henry III., much work seems to have been executed here, especially in the latter part of his reign. Great part of the outer wall of the inner ward, or old bailey, together with part of that on the eastern side of the outer bailey, including the north-east tower at the end of the foss, as well as the great hall, or what Treswell called the Queen's tower; probably also the Gloriette, and some portion of the walls of the middle and inner bailies, seem to have been erected in this reign.

In 5th Hen. III., Peter de Mauley accounts at the exchequer for 7,000 marks, spent in works of the castle of Corfe, in the cost of the custody of Eleanor, the king's cousin, of the daughters of the King of Scotland, and of Richard, the king's brother. Also for costs incurred by several visits of King John to Corfe, after Lewis, son of the King of France, came to England.†

12th Jan., 7th Hen. III. The sheriff of Dorset and Somerset was commanded to cause to be repaired the apartments *(domus)* of the king's castle of Corfe, and he was authorised to expend thereon the sum of £13 15s. 6½d. which shall be accounted to him at the exchequer.‡ The expenditure of this sum is included in his account of disbursements for this year.§ 11th Hen. III., the sheriff is authorised to expend 20 marks in the repairs of the apartments of the castle,‖ and he enters this item in his

---

* Pipe Roll. † *Ibid.* ‡ Close Roll, 7th Hen. III,
§ Pipe Roll. ‖ Liberate Roll.

disbursements for this year.* Very extensive new works were carried on at the castle towards the middle and close of this reign, as appears by the accounts rendered at the exchequer by succeeding sheriffs of the county.

20th Hen. III. The sheriff accounts for £291 10s. 2½d. for laying down joists and floors, and for leading in the tower of Corfe Castle, and £62 for making two good walls in the place of the palisades at Corfe, between the old bailey of the said castle, and the middle bailey, towards the west, and between the tower of the same castle and the outer bailey, towards the south.† The first of these two walls is scarcely now distinguishable amongst the ruins, some additions having been subsequently made, called the "New Bulwark," and the general arrangement being altered.

The second wall must either have been carried along at the base of the acclivity from east to west, near the site of the existing foss, an arrangement which the wording of the record seems to indicate, though it is difficult to reconcile it with the material evidence still subsisting: or else it might possibly have been the curtain wall which runs up the face of the hill from the second gateway to the keep. That this latter wall was not erected simultaneously with the adjoining gateway is apparent from the junction in the masonry, so far as it can be distinguished through the mass of ivy which, unfortunately, almost conceals it from view. It seems also to have been erected subsequently to the construction of the approach to the new bulwark, before described.

3rd Feb., 23rd Hen. III., the sheriff of Hampshire is commanded to cause to be felled in the king's forest of Porchester, fifty oaks for the works of the castle of Corf, and to cause them to be taken to the port nearest to the said castle, and the *custodes* of the Bishopric of Winchester are ordered to cause to be cut, in the wood of the bishopric, in the Isle of Wight, which is nearest to the king's castle of Corf, a shipload of brushwood (*unam navatam busch*) and

* Pipe Roll. † Pipe Roll.

to be carried to the castle. 28th Jan., same year, the king commanded the constable of Corfe to lay down new joists, and make such other repairs as were necessary in the Tower of Corfe, and also to repair the turrets, (*turellos*) the sliding or movable bridge (*pontem collehis'm*),* the well and the dwellings (*domus*) of the castle. The sheriff of Dorset was ordered to appropriate sixty marks for the works of the castle, and to cause to be carried from the port nearest thereto, the timber sent by the sheriff of Hampshire.† The costs are included in his accounts of disbursements for this year.‡

4th Oct. in the same year the bailiffs of Southampton were commanded by the King to purchase *octo miliaria cere*, [whatever they were,] and to cause them to be carried to the castle of Corfe, for covering his dwellings ("*domos*") there. They were to be delivered to H. de Trublevill, the constable of the same castle.§

24th Hen. III., the following items of expenditure occur. For carrying to Corfe, timber which the sheriff of Southampton sent to the port nearest to the castle, 36s. For works done in the castle, 60 marks. For carrying timber from the forest of Blakemor, and lead from Wareham to Corfe for the work of the said castle, 66s. 7½d.

In the 26th Hen. III., £8 4s. were spent in repairs of the king's dwellings ("*domorum*") in the castles of Corfe and Sherborne, and in the succeeding year the following sums were accounted for. For repairing the bridge and outer gate of the bailey, and the tower of the castle and for other works within the same castle £33 11s. 3½d. For repairing the turrets and dwellings ("*in turellis et domibus reparandis*") of the same castle 106s. 8d. For carrying timber for the works and for the livery of Gerard the carpenter, who had 7½d. per diem for thirty-four weeks and one day, £15 4s. 6d.

* This may have been a "pont coulis," a bridge made to slide backwards and forwards across the open space. The drawbridge, afterwards in general use, was called a "pont levis."
† Liberate Roll. ‡ Pipe Roll. § Liberate Roll.

10th Mar., 28th Hen. III., the sheriff of Dorset and Somerset was ordered to cause the tower of Corfe Castle to be pargeted (*perjactari**) with mortar where needful, and the whole of it to be whitewashed externally (*exterius dealbari*), for which in 30th Hen. III. he charges 29s. 2½d.†
18th March, 28th Henry III., the sheriff was commanded to cause to be completed the King's Chamber in the castle of Corfe, and the gate of the same castle; and at the same time the bailiffs of Southampton were commanded to purchase fifteen chares of lead, four hundred oak boards, and fifteen thousand nails for making doors and windows in Corfe Castle, and they are to cause them to be carried to Wareham* In 30th Hen. III. the sheriff charges £121 5s. 4d. for carrying timber to Corfe for the works of the castle, and for the wages of carpenters, masons, and other operatives, and for finishing the works.†

During the succeeding twenty years there seems to have been a suspension of any extensive new works; but in the 35th Hen. III. the sum of £11 10s. was spent in felling and carrying timber for the works of the bridge; and in 36th Hen. III., the Forester of Gillingham was ordered by the King to allow the sheriff to take six oaks for the works of the King's chapels of Corfe and Dorchester;† and 40th Hen. III. the sheriff of the county was ordered to cause the dwellings ("*domos*") in the castle to be repaired where necessary.‡ Small sums were expended in repairs of the King's dwellings in the castle in 41st, 47th, and 52nd Hen. III. And in 45th Hen. III. the King commands Walter de Burgeis and Adam FitzPain, "custodes" of the bishopric of Winchester, to cause fifteen oaks to be cut, and carried by sea to Corfe for the works there. In the same year the sheriff of Dorset and Somerset was commanded to make a stable in a convenient place within the castle of Corfe large

---

* Liberate Roll.   † Close Roll,   ‡ Liberate Roll.

enough for twenty horses, and to repair the gates and bridge of the castle without delay.*

2nd April, 54th Hen. III., the King commanded that £100 should be paid by Thomas de Sancto Vigore, and the sheriff of the county, to Henry de Alemannia, his nephew (son of Richard, king of the Romans), and Alan de "Plokenet," custodes of the castle of Corfe, for work to be done there; and at the same time they were commanded to purchase £100 worth of corn and wine, and deliver them to the said Henry and Alan for victualling the castle.† In the same year (1270) the sum of £62 was allowed to Alan de "Plunkenet" for work done at the castle.‡

A shield sculptured on the outside of the semi-circular tower, near the north-east corner of the outer bailey, seems to prove that this part of the castle was the work which was erected during the constableship of Alan de Plukenet, and for which the last-mentioned item of expenditure was incurred. The shield—of which an engraving is given at page 52—is heater shaped, such as was common in the reign of King Hen. III., but more obtuse than usual. It is held up by two human hands issuing from the wall, and bears in relief, as an heraldic device, five fusils in bend; or, as it would anciently have been described, a bend engrailed. The family of "Plokenet" —the name is spelt in various ways— bore ermine, a bend engrailed gules.§ The ermine is not indicated on this shield; but it does not thence necessarily follow that the arms were not intended for those of Plukenet, for at this early period, and where the sculpture is somewhat rude, the ermine spots may have been regarded in the nature of a tincture, in which case they would not be represented, except when painted.‖ It is not unreasonable, then, to assign to this tower the date of 1269-70.

---

* Liberate Roll. † Liberate Roll, m. 7. ‡ Pipe Roll.
§ Nicolas's Rolls of Arms, Temp., Ed. ii., page 5, and Temp., Ed. iii., page 35.
‖ Hutchins, who blazons this coat five fusils in fess, assigns it to Marshal, Earl of Pembroke, but that Earl's arms are well known to be wholly unlike these. They are blazoned—Per pale or and vert, a lion rampant, gules. [Nicolas's Roll of Arms, Temp. Hen. III.]

The fortifications surrounding the outer bailey having thus, as I suppose, been commenced by King Hen. III., were carried on on an extensive scale and completed during the following reign. Some of the materials of which the walls are composed may assist us in proximately assigning to them a date. It appears from the Plea Roll of 6 Ed. I., that William Clavile brought an action against Elyas de Rabayne, then constable of the castle, for that on Monday, the morrow of Easter, 5 Ed. I., he had caused a quarry to be dug on the property of the said William, at Holne, and therefrom carried away stone for the works of the castle. The only species of stone to be met with on the estate at Holme is a dark red sand-stone, totally differing in its nature and colour from the other stone of which the castle is for the most part built. Much of this red sand-stone is apparent in the Butavant tower, and is occasionally visible in the face of the whole of the walls, which extend thence to the south-western tower of the outer ward, including also that tower itself. It may be inferred, therefore, that this part of the building, or some portion of it, was in the course of construction shortly before the time that this dispute arose.

The fabric rolls, described in the introduction, give the names of many of the apartments, and afford some insight into the cost of labour and materials at the period, from 8th Ed. I. to 3rd Ric. II.

The compotus of Richard de Bosco, constable of the the castle, 8th Ed. I., shows the expenses incurred day by day from the Feast of the Nativity of St. John the Baptist 8th Ed. I., 24th June, 1280, to the Feast of the Apostles, St. Philip and St. James, 9th Ed. I., 1st May, 1281. He accounts for fifty marks received from John de Cormayle, the former sheriff, and twenty marks received from him from the issues of the county. Total, £46 13*s.* 4*d.*

It seems that the fortifications surrounding the outer ward were in course of erection at this time, and the entrance gateway appears to have been just finished, the gates themselves being now put up. 200 lbs. of iron were purchased for the outer gate for 8s. 4d., and Adam Bureis, a smith, was paid 5s. for making thereof two great hooks and two hinges (*gunphos et vertinellos*) for the outer gate, and nails to fasten on the latter. Master Ralph Totewys, a stonemason, was paid 2s. for a week's work in preparing the places where the hooks should be fixed, and cutting the stone. Thirty-six free stones were purchased of Sir Peter[*] for the gate and bridge for 2s.; and John Catel was paid 3d. for the week's work in assisting Master Ralph in putting up the gates at night and taking them down (*ponere et deponere folias*). This fixes the date of the outer gate to the year 8th Ed. I., 1280. Twelve quarters of lime, bought at Poole, cost 7s. 2d.; carriage thereof by Ower to Corfe, 12d.; and four boys who placed it in the stable to protect it from rain had 2d. Ten quarters of lime were also brought from Wareham. A bridge was now built, or repaired, as four men were paid 2s. for four days work digging the foundation. A tiler (*coopertor*) received 15d. for working (repairing?) over the King's Chamber, the chapel, the Queen's Chamber, and the chamber called Gloriet, and over the gate before the great tower, and over the other dwellings ("*super alias domus*") of the castle where requisite. New joists and floors were laid down in the great tower; and the prisons called Malemit and "Swaluwe" were cleaned out. 15d. were paid for hauling timber from the fosse next the middle gate to the King's Hall. 20d. was paid for four hired carts which brought timber from Studland. This is one of the very rare instances in which timber, apparently grown in Purbeck, was used about the castle. Carpenters were employed in felling timber in the wood of Lichet. A partition of lath and plaster was made (*in plastro faciendo*) between the long hall and the chamber.

---

[*] This was, no doubt, Peter Doget, called also "Dominus Petrus de Corf Capellanus," who had property in the neighbourhood, and was chaplain of the chapel of Corfe.

Three men were paid for a day's work, taking lead and boards from the great tower. William, the plumber, was paid 20s. for leading two towers, and William Borde received 2s. 6d. for cleaning out the great tower. The tower called Butavant was at the same time cleaned out, and candles were purchased to see by, which shews there was an oubliette, dark chamber, or dungeon in this tower. Richard Alymer, the carpenter, had 2s. for eight day's work flooring the tower called Butavant. 10th Ed. I., spike nails were made to fasten the boards to the joists over the same tower. Joists were provided to support the lead of this tower as well as those called Cocaygne and Plenteye. £18 3s. 8d. were paid to Robert Fitz John for lead for all three of the said towers. Thus we ascertain their proximate date, for they seem to have been completed about this time.

Twenty-three pieces of lead were purchased of Robert Fitz John for the chamber of the King and Queen, and a master plumber began to cover with lead by task-work the said chamber, for which he received £3. This shews that the chamber, wherever situated, was immediately under the lead roof. Edward Brandon received 1s. 4½d. for taking down by task-work the wall above the chamber next the chapel, and two masons were paid for making another wall next the King's chapel. Two men were paid 10d. for four days for cleaning the King's Chamber and the Queen's Chamber. Two coverers (tilers) were paid for repairing the Queen's Chamber and the chamber of the constable, and two who repaired the chapel of S. Mary, the kitchen, and the chamber beyond the stairs (*ultra staeria*). Thus it is shown that this chapel was in a part of the building covered with stone tile.

Amongst other expenses of 10th Ed. I. are the following items:—For ninety-two pieces of timber coming from Hampshire, landing the same at Ore, and carrying them to Corfe, £5 9s. For the expenses of brother Henry going to Twyford and remaining there to prepare the said timber, and returning therewith 22s. 1d. Also for his expenses in felling wood in Berewood (near Portsmouth) for a whole week, with one carpenter, 2s. 3d. He was the surveyor, master carpenter, or builder. A boy was paid 1s. 1½d. for going to Cerne, Godmanston, and Dorchester, in quest of carpenters. Hemp was bought to make a rope for hauling timber, and 3d. was paid for making the same at Studland. For three quarters of lime, bought at Bindon, 21d. For carriage of the same to the castle, 6d. To two sawyers, who sawed four joists for the tower called "Plante," for one day, 6d. For four cords made of hemp, bought for raising the bridges of the castle, 7s. 6d. For five locks, bought for the four gates of the castle and for the wine-cellar, 2s. 7d. For stone bought (*velutis petris emptis*)* of Henry Cusyn, for the towers which are called Butavant, Cokayngue, and Plente, 9s. For three hundred laths, bought at Wareham, for repairs of the apartments of the castle in parts, and for the new chamber beyond the gate, 2s. To William, the plumber, for a gutter newly made between the King's hall and the tower called Plenty, 3s.

Total expences of the work, 10th Ed. I., in purchase and carriage of timber, lead, stone, and lime, and wages of carpenters, masons, and other operatives, £81 8s. 1d.

From accounts of expenses incurred between the Feast of St. Cuthbert the bishop, 20th March, 13th Ed. I., and the Feast of St. Andrew the apostle, 30th Nov. following, it is found that they had at length begun to burn lime at Corfe instead of fetching it from Poole, Bindon, &c.† Fivepence were paid for cutting wood for burning lime "*in uno rogo*,'

---

* This kind of stone is frequently mentioned in these accounts. What was its character has not been determined. Possibly it might be squared flag or paving stone, from the French *velter* to guage or measure.

† From the fact that lime was, at different times, procured from Bindon, Sturminster, and Poole, the two first of which places are situated near the chalk district, and all three are far away from the limestone formation, it would seem that chalk-lime was then used in the castle works; and it may therefore perhaps, be inferred that when at length lime was burnt at Corfe, chalk, which was close at hand, was the material made use of.

and 19s. 6d were paid for the carriage thereto of seventy-seven cartloads of brushwood, at 3d. per cartload; the lime-burner had 8s. 4½d. Soon after this, however, there is a charge for lime from Poole.

A tiler (*coopertor*) was paid 5½d. for a day's work over the King's hall; and a man received 8d. for drawing five hundred stones for covering the dwellings (*domus*) in the castle. For the wages of a man ("*cooperientis*")—*i.e.*, repairing the tiling, over the chamber called the Gloriet, over the chapel and elsewhere in divers places, by task-work, 23d. For the services of a mason making two windows in the wall, for fixing a door ("*hostiam*") towards the little chamber within the King's chamber, 1½d. 6s. 8d. were paid for the wages of a painter ("*pictoris*") for whitewashing, &c. ("*dealbantis et listiantis*) the chamber of the King and Queen by task-work; and a man who brought water and lime to his hands had 2s. 3d. for three weeks. Walter Mogga had 1s. 6d. for carving free stones for the stair before ("*ad staeriam ante*") the chapel of St. Mary, in the upper dungeon ("*in superiori dungeon*"). He also received a like sum for carving stones for the steps leading to the tower and for laying them down there, and at the door of the hall. 12s. were paid for four hundred free stones purchased at Quarr.

Two carpenters who made and mended the outer bridge had 5s. 3d.; two sawyers sawing planks and joists for the same, had 2s. 8d.; and 3s. 6d. were paid for the service of two carpenters flooring the bridge and felling wood for a "trestell," preparatory to an expected visit of the King.

To John Spure and Geoffry, the carpenters who laid down joists and floors (*gistaverunt et planchiaverunt*) in Cokayne, 3s. 6d. To Robert Rudel, who assisted John Spure in laying down floors ("*planchias*") in the tower called Sauveray, for one day, 3d. For the service of a tiler who repaired the tiling ("*unius coopertoris qui cooperiebat*") over the upper chambers ("*sumas cameras*"), above the kitchen, the bakery and elsewhere, where necessary, for the week, 18d.

To Walter Mogga, a mason, for making a window between the chapel and the King's great chamber, and for doors "(*hostia*")" in the long chamber, by task, 9s. 6d., and for repairing a chimney in the long chamber, 2s. To John Alfrenton, and Robert Brende, and their brothers, for mending the wall next the King's Chamber and the kitchen, 4s. 6d.

A mason received 51s. 1d. for making a wall with a sewer ("*cum cloaca*") by task-work, on the west side of the outer gateway.

For the service of Geoffry Puddying going to Wudemannecote to apprise R. de Bosco, the constable, that the sheriff does not pay any money for the works, 9d. He also had six pence for going to the sheriff, who was then at Bristol, with letters from John de Kyrkeby (a Baron of the Exchequer) and R. de Bosco, no doubt, on the same business.

To Stephen, the plasterer ("*daubator*") who pargeted ("*perjactavit*") the long chamber next the tower, and the two chambers adjoining thereto, and also the oriel ("*orriolum*") before the King's chapel, by task work, 5s. 6d. To Peter Raymond, and John, his son, who made walls of plaster in the lesser constabulary and in the great tower, 2s. For one thousand stones bought for covering the dwellings ("*domos*") 2s. 3d. For two stone of hemp for ropes, for the bridge and well, 21d., and for the man who made the same ropes, 12d.

To John Wakeman, and Geoffry, the carpenters, for making windows between the chapel and the King's Chamber, and for boards outside ("*ultra*") the Queen's Chamber, 2s. 11d. For a lock for the same window, 3d. For tack nails for fixing the boards over the outer chamber ("*cameram forinsecam*") of the King and Queen, 1½d.

To the same carpenters, for making windows, hanging and fixing them, and also for making wickets ("*wikettas*") for the cistern and for the prison called Malemit, 3s.

To William Cok, who cleaned up the area before the King's Chamber and elsewhere, for four days, 5d. This looks as if the King's Chamber was on the ground floor. For tallow purchased for the works which were carried on at night, preparatory to the expected arrival of the King, 6d.

From the items of account between Palm Sunday, 18th Ed. I., 1290, and the Feast of Pentecost, 19th Ed. I., 1291, it appears that the western chamber, next the Queen's chamber, was lengthened eight feet, and a new gable and a new window were made. Also a new eastern chamber was built—viz., a new wall towards the north, two windows and a chimney were constructed, and three marble columns were carved for the same three windows. This shows that the windows were each of two lights, separated by a central shaft of Purbeck marble. The rooms are spoken of as "*novas cameras*," but from the context they seem to have been only partially newly built, replacing others which had stood on the same sites, some of the old wall and timber being taken down. These rooms seem to have adjoined the apartment called the Gloriette, a charge being entered for taking down the wall of the said two chambers and of the "Gloryette." The two chambers thus rebuilt were covered with lead, there were therefore no apartments over them. John Lenard had 2s. 6d. for carrying stone from Quarr, from whence also were procured eighty feet of tablement, or stringcourse, ("*tabulamenti*") which cost 3s. 4d. Four quarters of coal were now brought from Newcastle on Tyne, no doubt for making lime, at £1 per quarter.

20th Ed. I., fourteen chares of lead, price 44s. per chare, were purchased and brought from Wareham, for covering the two new chambers, and Cock, the plumber, had £4 for founding the same. Colours called "redying" and "rugeplum" were brought from Salisbury for ornamenting the walls of the chamber.

The next roll is dated 21st Ed. I., 1293, and relates to the cost of the work done in the castle and in the tower of

Corfe. Separate mention of the two is noteworthy. Wakeman and Alymer, the carpenters, were paid for making an outer chamber in the upper new chamber, in a different place from what was originally intended *(facientes forinsecam cameram in suma nova camera in alio loco quam prius provisum fuit).*

John le Wayte received 12d. for cleaning out the dwellings or apartments of the tower *(pro domibus turris mundand'),* and Richard Burgeis had 9s. 8d. for whitewashing the two new chambers, against the expected arrival of the King, who was there on Saturday, 12th September, in this year.* £19 3s. 3¾d. were paid for making a pit *(puteum)* by task-work, for burning lime. The sum of the cost of works done in the castle of Corfe in this year over and above those done in the tower of the same castle amounted to 51s. 10¾d.

Then comes an enumeration of the costs of rather extensive works done in the castle and tower of Corfe, especially on the summit of the great tower. John le Mere was paid £8 6s. 8d. for raising by task-work the wall of the chapel and of the chamber next *(juxta)* the King's Chamber, and for making a new chimney in the said chamber, also for making battlements ("*kernellos*") and copings or finials, ("*crastas*") for the said chapel and chamber. For stone corbels for the same work 20s. were paid. Five shillings were paid for stones for making "le Gareyt" over the same work.† William, the plumber, of Winchester, was paid 60s. for founding twelve chares‡ of lead, at 5s. per chare, for covering the said chapel and chamber. These items seem to prove that the chapel and the chamber here mentioned must have been immediately under the roof; and yet a charge is at the same time

---

* Itinerary of King Ed. I. MS. in Public Record Office.

† The Garytte (from the French "Guerite") was a term of fortification applied to a watch-tower or lookout place on the roof. [*Professor Willis's Glossary.*]

‡ A "chare" was a measure of lead. It contained thirty "pigs," each "pig" containing six stone wanting 2 lb., and every stone being 12 lb.

entered for a week's labour of two men carrying lime to the door of the King's chapel, for the wall of the chamber then existing above, the same chapel (*ad murum camere supra capellam Domini Regis existentem*). I think the "King's Chapel" was not the same as "the Chapel of St. Mary in the Tower."

Walter, the tiler (*coopertor*), of Wareham, was paid 20s. task-work for repairing (*cooperientem*) defects in the tiling of the dwellings ("*domorum*") of the castle in places—viz., the long chamber, near the King's chamber, and the apartments on the inner side of the outer gate. He was also paid for repairing the hall and constabulary. Fourpence was spent in two locks for the doors of the chamber called the 'Gloriette.' 6s. 8d. was paid for taking down the whole of the old lead from the tower. William Wall, the plumber, had £11 12s. 4d. for founding forty-six and a-half chares of lead, of which twelve chares came by sea from London, and thirty-four chares were from the old lead with which the tower was before covered. Robert Brind was paid by task-work £6 13s. 4d. for building up (*facientem*) the middle wall of the tower to the height of the timber; and John Trygge received 4s. for carving corbels for the said wall. 13s. 4d. were the wages of Robert Brinde for raising the wall of the tower on the four sides from the height of three feet under the timber ("*levantis murum Turris per quatuor partes ex altitudine trium pedum sub meremio*").

This, amongst other items, comes under the head of "*custus novarum domorum et murorum Turris castri de Corf.*"

The masonry of the interior of the south wall of the keep, as it now stands, shows the original weather mouldings of a ridge and valley roof of two bays, with a gutter between them, which must have originally covered what was then the highest floor, the walls being carried up all round to the height of the ridge of the roof. This roof appears to have been at some subsequent time removed, and the central wall being raised, an additional or third floor was constructed, surmounted by a lead flat. Alterations of this kind were not uncommon in Norman keeps, but they were usually made rather early within the period of Norman architecture. It is somewhat uncertain, therefore, whether this was the sort of work which was done on the occasion just mentioned.

The repairs and alterations seem now for the present to have been completed, for 21st June in the last mentioned year—viz., 21st Ed. I., the Barons of the Exchequer were commanded to pay to Richard de Bosco, the constable, £49 13s. which he had laid out in the works of the castle between Palm Sunday, 18th Ed. I., and the Feast of the Purification, 19th Ed. I. and £32 6s. 5d., which he had expended in a similar way between the last-named day and the same festival, in 20th Ed. I. Also £45 5s. 2¾d., which he had laid out in repairs of the dwellings ("*domorum*") of the castle in the last-named year; and 51s. 10¾d. in similar repairs; and £140 6s. 7d. for repairs and improvements (*in reparatione et emendatione*) of the tower of the castle, in 21st Ed. I.*

7th Jan. 31st Ed. I., the King commanded the sheriff of the county, out of the proceeds of his bailiwick to deliver to the Abbot of Milton, £50 for repairs of the bridge of the castle of Corfe.†

Some trifling repairs were made in 15th Ed. II., and amongst the items of expenditure 2d. were charged for a carpenter making bars for the doors of the tower, and of the prison in the dwelling ("*domum*") next the middle gate, for the safe custody of the prisoners. Also 8d. for repairs of a certain apartment beyond the gate (*quadam domo ultra portam*); and 1d. for a lock for the same. A carpenter was paid 3d. per diem for repairing the bridge and the dwelling beyond the middle gate; and a tiler ("*tegulator*") was employed to tile the same dwelling ("*domum ultra portam forinsecam*").

* Liberate Roll.   † Close Roll.

19th Ed. II., the King issued a writ, dated 15th Dec., and addressed to William de Blaneford, John de Brideport, and Walter Baril, reciting that he had committed to John Peche the custody of the castle of Corfe and the warren of Purbeck, during pleasure, in the same manner as others had held it; and willing to know the state of both, heretofore and now, he directs them, or any two of them, to survey the castle and warren, and inquire by a jury concerning the premises. In pursuance of this writ an inquisition was taken at Corfe on the 17th January following by a jury, who say upon oath that the King's hall in the said castle is decayed (*decesa*) to the damage of one hundred marks— viz., part of the said hall, in the time of Simon de Montacute, to the value of ten marks; in the time of Henry de Lacy, Earl of Lincoln, seventy marks; in the time of Robert Fitz Payne, custos of the said castle, twenty marks. The tower called "Cocangue" was damaged in the time of Roger Damery, custos, to the value of 100*s*. The chapel of St. Mary within the third gate, and the gate itself, was damaged in the time of Henry de Lacy, Earl of Lincoln, custos, to the value of £40. The long hall was decayed in the time of the said Earl to the value of eighty marks. A certain chamber called "*Le Parlour*," and the "*porchea*" before the chamber of the Queen ("*ante cameram Regine*,") was damaged in the time of the said Earl to the value of £20. The high tower, with the chambers and gardrobes in the same, were damaged to the value of £100— viz., in the time of Simon de Montacute, 100s.; in the time of Henry de Lacy, Earl of Lincoln, £40.; in the time of Robert Fitz Payne, £30; in the time of Richard Level, 100s.; in the time of Roger Damery, £20. The gate which is called "Middelghete" was damaged in the time of Roger Damery to the value of 100*s*. The great outer gate, and the bridge before it, were damaged in the time of the said Earl, £200. The window shutters *(ostia fenestrarum)* with the ironwork of the windows *(cum ferra-*

mentis fenestrarum) and the lead, in divers places of the castle were carried away to the damage of £20, viz, in the time of Simon, 40s.; in the time of the said Earl, £10; in the time of Robert Fitzpayne, 60s.; in the time of Richard Lovel, 20s.; in the time of Roger Damery, £4. As to the warren, they say it is well kept, and they know of no transgressions done there. They also say that in the castle are no arms nor victuals.—Total damage, £510.

In 14th Ed. III., the king issued a commission dated 22nd May, to Walter Rodeneye, John Comyn, and Robert Martin, reciting that he had been given to understand that the walls of his castle at Corfe, in Purbeck, were ruinous and required extensive repairs. Wishing to be certified of the truth thereof, he commands them to proceed in person to the castle, to survey the same and to inquire by a jury the extent of the said defects, at what time, by whose neglect, and how and in what manner they have arisen, and who is bound to repair them.* We meet with no account of any action having been taken in consequence of this commission, but in 30th Ed. III., there is a fabric roll which gives a minute account of carpenters' and blacksmiths' work, and includes the purchase of timber and the carriage of it from Wareham and Wimborne Holt, together with the purchase or manufacture of iron, joists, boards, nails, hinges, doors, windows, and shutters. The works were being pressed forward in anticipation of a visit from the king, which was expected shortly to take place.

Twenty-four pieces of oak timber were bought at Wareham, for joists for the King's Chamber, next the kitchen in the Gloriet, and for the gardrobe annexed thereto, and two carpenters were paid for working about the repairs of the said chamber, for which new windows† were at the same time made. The adjoining "*latrinæ*" were almost newly made.

* Rot. Pat. 2 pars. m. 31 in dorso.
† No doubt window frames or shutters.

Two lbs. of grease, price 4d., were bought for greasing the outside of the windows of the King's chamber on account of the heat of the sun. This probably relates to greased linen used instead of glass.

Fourteen doors and two leaves of a (folding) door for the entrance of Gloriet, and thirty-three window shutters (*folia fenestrarum*) were made; twelve of such doors, and nineteen window shutters being now placed in the King's chambers in the Gloriet and elsewhere. Seven shutters of the old windows, without hinges, and two old leaves of a door, at the entrance before the chapel of the Gloriet, together with six old locks, without keys, were found in the castle.

The floor boards in the High Tower and elsewhere were repaired, and the High Tower, the King's Chamber, abovementioned, Butavant and Cokayne, and other chambers in the castle were cleaned out.

The rubbish about the foundations of the bridge of the middle ward was cleared away, that the defects might be better seen. Eight great oaks, were purchased at Wymborn Holt, for newly making the bridge of the middle ward, but as a temporary expedient in expectation of the king's visit, fourteen pieces of oak timber were purchased to support it, and for rails, as it was in a weak condition. Carpenters were employed on the work.

In the week in which the Nativity of the Blessed Virgin fell, the carpenters' work was suspended on account of the king's visit, which then took place.

On this occasion three hundred pounds of iron, for which 24s. were paid, were bought at Southampton, conveyed by water to Ower, and thence to the castle, after which it was taken to Wool, near Bindon, to be there made into hooks and hinges ("*gumfos et vertiellos*") for the doors and windows. The king being shortly expected, a man, on horse-back, was sent in haste to Salisbury for two hundred nails, with tinned heads, for the window shutters. He was paid for his journey 1s. 6d. The nails cost 20d. Five hundred nails of a similar kind were also procured. Great spike nails, locks, and keys were bought at Woodbury. Four great locks with keys, cost 4s.

Some repairs were still being carried on in the 31st, 32nd, 36th, 38th, 41st, and 50th Ed. III. In 31st Ed. I., three pieces of timber were purchased at Corfe and used about the middle ward, called le Butavant, and about the fountain. Two pairs of double hinges were provided, one of which was for the prison called Butavant, and the other for the fountain. Sand was brought from Blachenwell.

A fabric roll of 36th and 38th Ed. III., relates to the purchase and carriage of timber from the New Forest and elsewhere, and of lead and other materials, the wages of carpenters, masons, and others. There seems, however, to have been but little masonry done at this time. Amongst the items are as follows:—Two men for two days had 12d. for pulling down the old kitchen. Two masons were employed for nine days in making a wall round the kitchen, *circa coquinam*. Timber was bought at Bestwall for renewing the laths of the kitchen; eighty oaks were purchased at Beuleu, and other timber was bought of William Chick, of Wareham, for new making the kitchen. The principal carpenter hired to new make the kitchen, and to make the gates of the outer and higher wards, had 21s. for forty-three day's work. Crests were also procured for the kitchen. Twenty shillings were paid for tiles for covering it, and 12s. were paid for tiles for the other buildings. The carriage of both lots cost 8s. 6d., and tilers were paid for putting them on. Sixpence was paid for the carriage of twelve stones (corbels) for the kitchen, for supporting the timber. Timber was purchased for repairing a certain chamber next the Gloriet, and for making a certain wardrobe next to "Botifant." A smith was paid for making "*hokes and twysten and crampons*" for the chimneys of the Gloriet.

In the 41st Ed. III., under the constableship of John de Elmerugg, William de Clavyll and Thomas de Estoke were surveyors of the works of the castle, when various repairs were effected. The High Tower was newly roofed with timber and lead, and the tower called Cokeyn was repaired both in the lower and upper floor, and newly covered with lead. The tower called Plente was also newly covered with lead, and the timbers of the upper floor were renewed. A little stable was newly built in the lower ward, and a little kitchen, next the outer gate, was thoroughly repaired. A great piece of timber, thirty feet long, was bought for the High Tower. One thousand seven hundred and fifty tiles were purchased for the roofs of the buildings, *(domorum,)* and two masons were paid for six days in newly building the walls of the kitchen. The cost of the whole amounted to £134 3s. 1d. On this occasion, timber from "Beuluwe," (Beaulieu, in Hampshire) was brought by sea to Ower, some came from Wareham, and some from Wimborne Holt. Lead was brought from London, and lime was at different times brought from Wareham, Lulworth and Sturminster.

Robert Wantynge, parson of the church of Radclyve, accounted for £67 4s. 10d., expended by him in repairs of the castle in pursuance of the king's writ, dated 27th Nov., 50th Ed. III. The works consisted for the most part of mason's work about the walls, apparently the external walls of the castle. Four boards called "wainescote" were purchased for molds for the stone masons, price 6d. Six men were employed for sixty days pulling down the stone of the walls and preserving the free-stone thereof,* and twenty more were similarly employed for the same number of days in saving the same stones from being broken.

Four masons *(positores*, setters) had 5d. a day each, for 14 days for making a lime kiln *(puteum pro crematione calcis)*. Eight quarriers had each 4½d. a day for eighteen days digging stone, and eight rough masons had 6d. a day for

---

* This relates to the ashlar, the interior of the walls being formed of chalk and rubble.

ninety-two days for forming the same for the walls. Two masons *(positores)* were paid 5d. a day for forty-three days.

Stone was now used for lime instead of chalk, and three labourers were employed for forty days digging "*lymestone*," in the quarry, to be burnt into lime. Each being paid 4½d. a day. Eight other labourers had 3d. a day for sixty days, for breaking the stone preparatory to its being burnt. Forty quarters of sea-coal for burning the lime, cost 100s. Forty-five cart loads of brushwood, used for the same purpose, cost 8d. per load. Ten labourers were employed in cutting the same underwood and making an enclosure after it was cut, in the king's wood, called "Kingeswood."*

In this account no particular parts of the castle are specified, except the chapel, for the mending of the glass windows of which 41s. were paid.

In 51st Ed. III., a new bridge was built, the foundation and piers whereof were of stone, and the superstructure of timber. The latter was brought from the forest of Gillingham, and stone was procured from Lynch.

Between 1st November 1st Ric. II. and 3rd Nov. in the following year, a new tower called la Gloriet, within the castle, containing five chambers, was built, and £269 6s. 2d. was expended. Timber was again brought from Gillingham, and stone from Quarr, in Purbeck. Twenty quarters of sea-coal were bought at Wareham for burning stone for lime.

From these fabric rolls we obtain some interesting facts relating to the cost of construction, and the source from whence the materials were acquired. It will have been seen that in the time of Ed. I., the wages of carpenters were 2½d. or 3d. per day; masons had 3d. or 4d.; tilers and sawyers had 3d.; labourers 1d. or 2d., according to the skill or capabilities of each; boys got 1d. per day, and women the same, or sometimes only 4d. per week. The surveyors of the work had 1s.

† This shows that the woods in Purbeck were unınclosed, except that after the underwood was cut a temporary fence was made round the spot to protect the young growth from being browsed by deer and cattle,

per week. For lime from Bindon 9d. per quarter was charged, but from Poole it was only 4½d. In 14th Ed. I. they had begun to burn it on the spot, and coal from Newcastle used for that purpose cost £1 per quarter. The lime seems to have been sometimes made of chalk, but latterly lime-stone was certainly used. The extraordinary hardness and durability of the mortar with which the castle is built—some of which has proved to be even more durable than the stone itself—makes it interesting to see how the lime was burnt and from whence the material was procured, though, no doubt, much of the strength of the mortar is due to its having been used in a liquid state, and poured in while hot. Lead cost forty-four shillings a "chare," and iron ½d. a lb.; stone 2½d. a load. The hire of a cart and team was 6d. per day, but the hire of a riding-horse 1½d. Much of the work was done as task-work. The greatest part of the timber came from the New Forest or from Bere Forest, near Portsmouth; but some, in 30th Ed. III. was brought from Holt, in Dorsetshire. Studland was the only place in Purbeck which supplied any, and that but once. Possibly it may have been landed there from Hampshire. It would thus seem that Purbeck was not then much more productive of oak timber than it is at present. The timber was used green, as soon as it was fell'd. There is no mention of glass in any of these accounts, except for the chapel, and that is not found till so late as 51st Ed. III. The shutters of the windows are continually spoken of and the absence of any mention of glass for such windows leads to the conclusion that none was used except for the chapel.

An undated MS., in possession of Mr. Bankes, the present owner of the castle, apparently in the hand-writing of the 16th century, and headed, "A Particular of the Castell and Maner of Corfe," describes it as "a very fayre castell with a gatehouse, with fayre rooms, &c., inclosed with a great stone wall, with ground containing about six acres for gardens and walks." At this time, therefore, it seems that the several wards had been converted into something like pleasure grounds.

King Henry VII. repaired this castle for the residence of his mother the Countess of Richmond, and 2,000*l.* were granted by Parliament for that purpose; but it is not known that she ever resided here. Coker says, "Sir Christopher Hatton much repaired it and amended it, being almost overcome by time;" and at one or other of these periods the several square-headed windows which are still visible in the keep were probably inserted.

The following description of the castle forms part of "A Relation of a Short Survey of the Westerne Counties, &c.," 1635, "by a captaine, lieutenant, and an ancient, all three of the military company in Norwich.*

"It is so ancient as without date, yet all her walls and towers, the maine castle called the King's, the lower castle called the Queen's, the large roomes therein, and the leads aloft, are all in very good repayre. After I passed over the bridge that crosseth that deep dike south from the towne I entered into a large and spacious court (wherein and on the platform next the Queen's castle, lye mounted towards the gate some pieces of ordinance), by which I ascended through another strong gate-house into the inner court, and so with a winding ascent up into the great hall of the King's castle, the guard chamber, and the rest.

"The walls round about her are very strong and large, and have faire walkes, secure platforms, and good ordinance, but their chiefest guns, wch were goodly brave brasse pieces, were lately battered and broken to pieces and sold by one (you may imagine†) rather of Venus than Mars his company, much to the weakening of the whole island."

The following inventory of stores and furniture, delivered over for the King's use by Thomas de Bridport, lieutenant

---

* Lansdowne MS. 213. † The Lady Hatton.

of Sir Philip de Weston, late constable of Corfe Castle, to Philip de Baglee, lieutenant of Sir John Grey of Ruthyn, the then constable, in the feast of St. Simon and St. Jude, 20 Edw. III. 1346, gives us but a mean idea of the extent to which a great fortress was supplied and furnished in the middle of the fourteenth century, viz.: "22 quarters of wheat, strike measures, 27 quarters of oats, half a carcass of salt beef, and 5 carcasses and 2 quarters of ditto, 60 carcasses of salted muttons, of which 30 were putrid, 19 small bacons, 8 tuns (*dolia*) of red Gascony wine, 11 tuns of white wine, 1 tun ot old and weak wine of the fifth year (*de quinto folio*), 8 quarters of coarse salt, 1 rick of hay, estimated at 12 cart loads, 2 empty tuns (*dolia*), 2 open tubs (*tunas*), 1 hanging bell for the chapel, 2 moveable tables, 1 dormant table broken and rotten, 4 pairs of trestles, 5 forms, 1 cupboard, 1 dresser for bread in the pantry, 1 wicker basket for holding bread, 1 dresser with four feet in the kitchen, 1 old dresser, 1 staddle to support barrels, 1 lead for the fountain (*pro fonte*), 1 lead fixed in the furnace (*fixum in fornace*), 1 brass basin of scarcely any value, 1 bucket bound with iron for drawing water, 1 brass pot without feet, 1 tripod, 1 hand saw, 1 barrel containing six lagens, 2 cords of scarcely any value, 2 old hawsers for working the drawbridge, 1 old cable for working the bridge, 2 cartloads of litter, 1 great net for catching large animals or wild fowl (*pro foris capiendis*, qu. *feris?*), 1 net called haye, 6 nets for catching hares, 4 ladders, 1 bier for the sepulchre in the chapel*, 2 pair of fetters (*gyves*), 37 old basenets of scarcely any value, 8 habergeons of scarcely any value, 1 iron chain and collar, 2 iron chairs (*ij. cathedras ferri*), broken and of scarcely any value, and 7 bows for arbalists of scarcely any value.

The same articles ot furniture, &c., described in nearly similar terms, in another inventory, had been delivered,

---

* In another inventory of the same effects, hereafter mentioned, this is called one sepulchre for Good Friday.

together with the custody of the castle, to Thomas de Bridport, by Walter Curpeton, lieutenant of Philip de Weston, on Good Friday in the same year, in the presence of Richard de Derneford, William Scovyle, Henry Smedemore, John Chanterel, John Attemill, William Canon, and Richard Huldeway.*

A comparison of this meagre catalogue with the following account of articles taken from the castle after its capture by the Parliament forces, will show the great change which had taken place in the social habits of the country between the 14th and 17th centuries. After the Restoration Sir Ralph Bankes endeavoured to ascertain what had been taken away, and into whose hands the furniture and other things had fallen. Various inquiries were made, and many of the articles were found; a few of the items are here given:

"One piece of ordynary hangings for ye gallery; one piece to hang behind the clossett and door in my La. chamber; one piece over the door going into the hall; and one neere to the doore in the studdy next to ye gallery.

"One piece of ordinary hangings for the door of the gallery.

"Two pieces of ffine tapestry for ye gallery: one piece to hang behind my La. bed.

"One piece for the lower end of the great chamber; one piece over the chimney in the great chamber.

"Two large sattin wrought window cushions; one cushion of crimson velvett for a window.

"A suite of green leather gilted hangings; one suite of blewe silke damaske hangings.

"A silke quilt carpett for ye table in the withdrawing room.

"A rich ebony cabbinett wth gilded fixtures; two mantles in red silke damaske, and a white silke damaske with 2 silver bindings."

* Miscellaneous Records in the Exchequer.

Then follow very numerous items of beds, carpets, and other descriptions of household furniture.

In another house in the country the same inquirer sees large store of articles from the castle, amongst others :—

"A trunk wherein is a crimson satten petticoat, with stomacher and sleeves lined with 6 silver laces, a sweet bag, a piece of silk stuff, and divers other small things"

Another person, employed to make inquiry in London, writes to this effect :—

"Stone, the broker in Barbican, had at his house a suite of forest worke tapestry hangings ; a green cloth bed embroyder'd with tent stitch slips of flowers, and lined wth Isabella coloured sarsanett. Also he said he had sold to a fine lord a tapestry suite of hangings of ye history of Astrea and Caledon, w^{ch}, I think, he said he had two or 300*l*. for.

The fine lord above mentioned appears, from the result of another inquirer's report, to have been the Earl of Manchester. This report from Barbican proceeds thus :—

"He had also a trunke with a black wrought work'd bed, and ye other furniture, besides cushions, and other things.

"All these things I saw, and ye bed my master treated with him to buy ; and he askt as dear for it as he paid.

"Also he said he had sold a hangings for a roome of rich watched damask, all of which, he said, he bought of Colonel Bingham ; and I think he said that he bought to the value of 1,000*l*. worth of goods of him."

The next memorandum is a paper indorsed in the handwriting of Lady Bankes, "about things lost in the castle," intituled, "The Goods lost in the Castle out of the Wardrop" :—

"7 or 8 suits of fine tapestry hangings.

"A suite of watchet damask hangings.

"A suite of green plush hangings.

"A suit of pentado hangings, and curtains and quilt.

"A furniture for a bed, and carpet, and quilt of green cloth embroydered with work.

"A white dimity bed and canopy, with the whole furniture wrought withe black.

"4 Turkey carpets with a white ground, 2 of them very long.

"8 other Turkey and Persia carpets, some long, some less sizes.

"A wrought quilt, white and yellow.

"A suite of scarlet and gilt leather hangings.

"Several trunks of linen, diaper, and damask, with NB., the other linen I^B M.

"Several trunks with flaxen sheets and table linen marked.

"A very large ebony cabinet.

"A very large trunke, inlay'd all over with mother of pearle.

"A trunke, with all sorts of fine child-bed linen, as sheets, and pillow-cases, and mantles.

"One of crimson plushe, with 2 fair silver and gold laces.

"One crimson damask mantle laced and divers others.

"Some crimson damask curtains, and long cushions for a couch.

"6 very fine and long down beds, with bolsters, and pillowes and blanckets.

"Several trunks of wearing clothes and wearing linnen.

"Many books and papers, at the value of 1,300*l.* all new and good, with many other things not mentioned.

"The goods which were about the castle :—

"A large suit of crimson velvet chairs, stooles, couch embroydered, long cushions of crimson velvet.

"Turkey carpets for the tables.

"2 furnitures for beds, one purple, the other crimson, with counterpoints, carpets, stooles, chairs.

"Stript hangings for 4 or 5 chambers.

"One suit ; 8 pieces of superfine dorcas, 12 foot deep ;

the story of Astrea and Caledon.

"A second suit of tapestry, 12 foot deep.

"A third suit of tapestry, the story of Constantine.

"A fourth, fifth and sixth suit, 12 foot deep.

"In a trunk, with letter Q :—

"One suit of hangings of rich Watchet damask, lined with blew cloth, 9 pieces, and one carpet.

"In a trunk marked with letter O :—

"A furniture for a bed of French green cloth embroyder'd; 6 curtains and valences, with changeable taffety teaster head-cloth and fringe, all of the same taffety; 2 carpets of cloth embroyder'd; an Indian quilt of white, wrought with yellow, to the bed.

"6 large down and five feather beds and bolsters.

"4 pair of down pilowes and quilts.

"5 pair of fine long blanckets.

"Fine linen particularly enumerated, in boxes numbered and lettered from A to the letter O."

The memorandum thus continues :—

"All these things before mentioned in particular, with many others not so well remembered, were layed up together in one roome in packes and trunks, and brought away, first to the Isle of Wight, and then to London, and most of the bed-hangings and other things sold to brokers, where some of them have been seen. There were besides lost in the castle all that which was in use about the castle: a suit of crimson velvet in the parlour; above 20 good feather beds and bolsters, pilows, blanckets, rugs, and furniture to them all; new and good hangings in several chambers; household linnen, new and good; all other necessaries of pewter, brasse, iron, tables, stooles, and all else belonging to a house; with many armes in the magazine and hall of S^r Jo. Bankes owne, all there, to the value of above 400l., pilledg'd by the souldiers."*

---

* Mr. Bankes's Story of Corfe Castle, pp. 250—254.

PRIVILEGES.

Considerable privileges were attached to the tenure of the castle and manor. The lord of the manor, who was in most cases the constable, was Lord Lieutenant and Admiral of the island, with power to array the militia.

Many of the farms in the island were charged with a certain number of bushels of wheat, to be annually rendered at the fortress. Every tything in Purbeck was bound to furnish an able-bodied man for ten days, in times of disturbance, for defence of the castle, at the king's cost, and men of Corfe were, by ancient custom, to keep watch in the castle in time of war, each receiving $\frac{1}{2}$d. per night.*

6th Edw. I., William de Clavill brought an action against Elyas de Rabayne, who was then the constable, for causing five oaks, belonging to the said William, to be felled at Holne, and carrying them to Corfe, and also for opening a quarry at Holne, and carrying stone from thence to Corfe. Elyas acknowledged the taking, and justifies on the plea that the constables had a right by custom to cut timber and dig stone throughout the warren for repairs of the castle. The jury, by their verdict, say that it was lawful for every constable of the castle to take timber for the repairs thereof when necessary, and that one of the six oaks was used for the repairs of the bridge, but the rest were appropriated by the said Elias as fuel for his own use. Damages to the

* Ministers' accounts.

amount of one mark are given for the five oaks and for the stone so taken. At the same time Elias de Rabayne, and others, were attached to answer to the Abbess of Shaftesbury for cutting and carrying away five hundred ashes, and two thousand maples and thorns in her wood at Kingston, whereby they damaged two hundred acres. Elias pleads the custom of the castle to take fuel from the said woods, but the jury say that, though the constables of the castle have in truth been accustomed to take from the uninclosed woods, in the vicinity of the castle, whatever was necessary for the works of the castle, and even for fuel in moderation, yet De Rabayne had taken it in a different manner from that which was customary with other constables, for he wasted 20 acres of the wood for his own use, and not for the repairs of the castle. He was therefore amerced.*

19th Ed. I., the king wishing to be informed concerning the true value of his castle of Corfe, and the chace there, issued his commission to Thomas de Marlebergh, dated 5 Feb., commanding him to proceed thither and cause the same to be extended. Thereupon, on Thursday next before the quinzene of Easter, 19 Edw. I. a jury was summoned, who say, amongst other things, that the easements of the houses and castle, and the pasture in the same castle, are of no value beyond reprises. There is one water mill there which is worth per annum 6s. 8d. There are thirteen free tenants in the town of Corfe holding small tenements, whose names, with the rent they paid, are then set forth; total rent, 36s. 7d. The mayor of Corfe has the pesage of wool and cheese, and of other merchandize, and pays per annum two pounds of wax, value 12d. Various persons, whose names are mentioned, hold cottages or tenements by small rents of cumin, wax, and horse-shoes, the latter rent being the most frequent; the value of each horse-shoe is reckoned at 1d. William Scovill pays the King one pound of pepper per

---

* Placita Assis., 6 Ed. I., Dorset m.7.

PRIVILEGES.   127

annum, worth 12d. for inclosing a certain place of meadow. The tenants of the Abbess of Shaftesbury, in Northdon, pay the King 20 horse-shoes, with the nails, at Michaelmas, value 20d. The tenants of Henry le Guldene, in Redlyngton, pay the same. Rents of assize at Newton to be paid by the burgesses, those of Whitsuntide and the yule of August and Michaelmas in equal portions, 2s. 6d.; 9d. rent is paid by the same burgesses at Michaelmas for placing their nets on the King's ground. The tenants of the Abbot of Milton in Ore pay 5s. at the Nativity of St. John the Baptist, and at Christmas, for having an easement for their cattle in the King's heath. Dionisia Stretche holds at Oulewell a certain tenement which was Joan de Bonevill's, and pays 20s. per annum. William de Moulham holds at Moulham a messuage and two virgates of land, rendering annually one load of hay, value 2s.; and he ought to find a carpenter to work about the Great Tower when our lord the King should wish it to be repaired, in case repairs are necessary, for which he is to receive of the King per diem 2d., or his board, such work over and above the said corrody is worth 1d. John Mautravers, John de Clavill, and William de Herston, render annually at the castle one load of hay, value 2s. Henry Talebot, William le Eyr, and John le Neuman, the same. Richard de Derneford renders there a cart-load of hay, value 12d. The tenants of John le Waleys in Middlebere render to the King annually two quarters of salt, value 2s. A similar rent is due by custom from divers tenants there making salt; also rents of 24 widgeons or hens, value 2s. There are three acres of meadow called Holewich, value per annum half a mark. The pasture called Castle Close, with the pastures around the castle, is worth by the year 70s. The pasture called King's Doune is worth per annum 2s.; "Placita Capituli," in the town of Corf, value per annum 2s.; pleas and perquisites of court of the same town, value 40s., with the heriots of the men of the new town. The pleas and perquisites of chace, except of venison, worth per annum 20s.; chiminage in the said chace worth per annum 2s. Item, there is a certain rent of 32s. to be paid at the feast of the Nativity of St. John the Baptist for the carriage of turves and other things as well at forbidden times as otherwise. The fees of prisoners and distresses coming to the castle, value per annum 12d. Item, the King has wreck of the sea, and it was this year worth 19s. in 100 lb. of wax. The keepers of the chace receive nothing of the King, but he pays wages to the constable and the porter.*

6 May, 2 Rich. II. the King issued a writ addressed to John Darundell, chivaler, John Mautravers, John Ways, and Richard Marleberghe, directing them to inquire by a jury as to all the lands, tenements, and liberties, together with their value belonging to his Castle of Corfe, which is ancient demesne of the Crown (*quod est de antiquo dominico coronæ*).†

In pursuance of the King's writ, bearing date 15 Novr. 4 Ric. II., a jury was summoned to inquire what possessions, rents, rights, customs, and liberties from ancient times belonged and then still belonged to the castle and lordship of Corfe, and whether any of them had been alienated, withheld, or neglected, and if so, then which of them, by whose default, when, and in what manner, to the damage and disinheritance of the King.

By an inquisition taken at Corfe Castle, on Monday next after the feast of St. Scolastica the Virgin (Feb. 10), 4 Ric. II., the jury say that all the underwritten liberties, rights, and customs belong to the said castle and lordship as contained in the Custumal of the castle, which was then in the custody of Philp Walwyn the constable, and was delivered to him by John Mautravers, his predecessor, and also in the Custumal of the town, written in an ancient hand, and found in the Missal of the parish church of Corfe, and that the same liberties, &c., have been exercised from time immemorial.

---

* Ministers' Accounts, Miscellaneous, in the Exchequer.
† Rot. Pat. 2 Rich. II. 2a pars, m. 13, a tergo.

That the whole Isle of Purbeck is a warren* of our lord the King and pertains to his said castle, and it extends from a path which is between Flouresberi and the wood of Wytewey and thence as far as Luggeford, from that to the bridge of Wareham, and so along the sea, in an easterly direction, to a place called the Castle of Stodland; thence by the sea-coast to the chapel of St. Aldelm, and from thence still by the sea-coast towards the west until it again reaches the aforesaid place of Flouresberi.

That the whole town of Corfe belongs to the said castle, and the tenants of the same town are called "barons," and ought to choose amongst themselves a mayor, coroner, and bailiffs, for whom they are willing to answer, and they are as free as the barons of the Cinque Ports. But so nevertheless that they ought not to hold any pleas except of " pepoudres " before the mayor, but to present and try all before the constable and his steward, to whom belong the amerciaments arising therefrom.

That all pleas of vert and venison, and also of wreck of sea, belong to the said castle, and ought to be decided by the constable and his steward, whereof all ransoms belong to the constable. And if any stranger, either of the warren or from any other place, should commit any trespass for which he should be attached within the bounds of the said liberty, by pledges, he should answer before the constable in due course of justice, so that no homager (*nullus homo*) ought to hold his court of the same plea.

That if any one of the vill of Corfe should have complained to the constable or mayor of Corfe against any one of the said warren, and to whomsoever of them gage or pledge

---

* The whole Isle of Purbeck was well stocked with deer. King John made it a forest, by which it became subject to the oppressive forest laws, but the *Carta de foresta* having been extorted by the barons from K'ng Henry III., the perambulators appointed to enquire what lands ought to be disafforested (viz., all such as had been afforested since the reign of King Hen. II.) reported that the Isle of Purbeck ought to be only a hare warren (*warenna ad lepores*) pertaining to the Castle of Corfe. It was in fact, however, a "chase," for the deer continued to range over the whole island down to the 17th century.

should have been given for a debt or other delict, he of the warren, whoever he may be, ought to be attached by the sworn warreners of our lord the King, and so appear and answer in the next ~~hundred~~ (court) in due course of law before the constable, saving to the constable the amerciaments accruing therefrom, so that no (other) person ought to have jurisdiction (*curiam suam habere*) in that business.

That our lord the King ought to receive a moiety of the profits of all causes belonging to the bishop or archdeacon throughout the whole parish of Corfe, and when the officials of the bishop or archdeacon shall have heard causes there they shall have liberty to hunt hares (*habebunt leporarios currentes ad lepores*) under super-vision of the warreners.

That if there shall be carts in the vill of Corfe capable of carrying a whole tun of wine (*dolium vini integrum*), the owners of such carts ought to carry at most two tuns of wine per annum to the constable, from Wareham to the castle, and those who shall have carried them shall have for each tun 4d. and their corrody honourably.

That the men of Corfe ought to receive at the bridge of Wareham prisoners sent to the castle by the mandate of the King, and to conduct them, with the aid of the constable, to the aforesaid castle, and when (such prisoners) are again delivered over to another prison, (the men of Corfe) ought to conduct them back to the before-mentioned bridge with the aid aforesaid.

That when there may happen to be war in the neighbourhood of the castle, the tenents of the town ought to be in the castle for forty days at their own charges for the defence of the same castle, and this as service for the tenure of their lands.

That the tenants of the town of Corfe ought to find a cart every Saturday to carry bread and beer from Wareham to Corfe for the use of the constable, and those who drive the carts shall have their corrody honourably from the constable, or 3d. in lieu thereof.

That the constable shall take assize of beer, viz., twelve lagens of beer for 3d. both within the town of Corfe and without it, throughout the whole warren, so (that is to say) that one half of the said assize should be beer of the best quality and the other half of second quality. If he should wish to have anything beyond this, he shall purchase it like other people.

That no merchant buying a fish within the warren ought to take it out of the warren or carry it away, unless he shall have placed it for sale at the cross of Corfe, delaying the sale of it for an hour of the day. And if he should do otherwise, and should be apprehended in flight, he shall forfeit his fish at the will of the constable.

That on every removal of a constable the warrener ought to summon four men of Bronkeseye to come to Corfe before the constable, and there in full hundred court make oath that they presume not to bring any malefactor within or out of the warren with their knowledge; and the men of Oure should do the same.

That the men who have woods of their own in the warren ought not to cut or carry away any such wood without the supervision of the warrener, except in the following case, (viz.,) if they shall ask leave of the warrener to take some, and they are not able to obtain permission, then they shall come to the gate of the castle with witnesses of the town, showing this to the porter and asking leave. If afterwards they should be attached (for taking wood), they shall be liberated without loss as soon as the premises (*i.e.* the groundless refusal of the warrener) shall have been proved.

That to the vill of Corfe belongs judgment by fire, water, and battle (*judicialia ignis, pola, et bellum*), and all pleas belonging to the King and the dignity of his crown, so that they ought to be determined there before the King's judges.

That the common council of the town ought to choose amongst themselves a mayor, coroner, and ale-tasters.

That no constable or warrener, except the warrener sworn

before the constable in full hundred court, ought to attach any man (found) with (wood) green or dry, (*cum viridi vel sicco,*) within the bounds of the warren or vill of Corfe, nor shall it be lawful for any one to attach any man carrying arms in the King's highway, unless the latter shall have committed some delinquency.

That the constable in the King's right, in respect of the said castle, has taken, time out of mind, prisage of wine of every ship coming to the sea coast of Purbeck, if it shall remain there, and shall have been moored there with cables and anchors, and if it shall have a freight or cargo of wine.

That the constable takes wreck of the sea throughout the whole of the bailiwick, time out of mind.

That our lord the King has taken, time out of mind, all royal fish, viz., grampuses, porpoises, and sturgeons, caught upon the coast.

That our lord the King also takes all falcons building and nesting within the said bailiwick, but the constable is accustomed to reward the captors of such fish and falcons.

That the liberty of the town of Corfe extends from the ditch on the east of Swyneswell, and so continuously on the west of the ditch of the land of Alfrington towards the south, as far as "la Wythie," and thence to the croft which Robert Scovill holds of our lord the King by service of 1 lb of pepper per annum. From the said croft, on the south of the meadow called Holewyssh, as far as a new ditch of William Elys, and thence to the ditch of William Grigge and John Bakere of Homerwell. From the same ditch to the water running from Blachenwell, and so along the water to Blachenwelle bridge; thence to the great thorn under the bank (*subitus bankam*), and so continuously beneath the same, as far as the stone standing in Litelmede; thence by la Lesedych to Shulford, and so continuously by the waters called Wychewater and Holewysshewater, following the stream to Spadefordbrugge;

That our lord the King has and used to have as appurtenant to his said castle all the meadow and pasture between Corfhayes and the manse of the parson of the church of Corfe, together with the pasture upon the hill, as far as the bounds of Nordone.

That common pastures everywhere within the liberty of Corfe, together with vacant lands (*terra vacua,*) belong to the tenants of the said town for their common use, and also the tenants shall have of the constable every night four lagens of beer whilst they shall keep watch within the castle in time of war.

That the mayor of the said town shall have pesage* everywhere within and without the liberty, throughout the whole of the said warren, for which he pays annually two pounds of wax at Michaelmas.

That the mayor every year in right of his office may have one lamb feeding in the pasture of our lord the King called Castle Close, quit of (payment for) herbage.

That when the parish church of Corfe Castle may have become vacant by the death of any parson, the King is used of old to present his clerk to the aforesaid church in right of his said castle, which presentation, however, the Abbess of Shaftesbury has appropriated to herself as in right of her manor of Kingston, in Purbeck, as it is said by the Abbess, but the right of the Abbess is unknown to the jurors.†

The following is from a M.S. volume at Kingstn Lacey, in the handwriting of the 16th century, which appears to have belonged to Sir Christopher Hatton.

"*Certaine Customes and Orders belonging to the Castle to be approved by the Court Rolles and com'on use.*

"1t^m· There appertayneth to the Castle of Corffe 2 lawdayes yearly to be kept at the castle gate, called the oute lawdayes, being of the nature of a wood courte, or

---

* *i.e.*, the exclusive right of weighing goods.
† Inq. 4 Ric. II. No. 128.

swannymote courte, the one kept at the ffeast of Saint Michaell the Archangel, the other at the ffeast of the Annunciation of our Ladye, whereunto doth appear all the freeholders of the island, and all the tithenge men of all the 2 hundreds of Roughbarrow and Hasillor, with there postes and sydmen, some with five, fower, three, or two, as appeareth by record.

"It^m. There are two usuall lawdayes for the towne kept at the termes and place aforesayde by the constable officer.

"It^m. The constable officer and steward may keepe every iiijth week a courte called hundred courte, wherein are tryed wrytts of right, pleas of trespas and debt, and all other common pleas. At their court be made presentments of offenders against the game and of veart, and wreake, by the raunger and wariners of Purbeck, as well in the lawedayes, wherein the wariner is the officer to execute proces and to present all measure, weights, and bruars and other offences.

"It^m. Every ffisherman within the iland, at every lawdaye payeth to the castle for licence to ffishe for every boat 4d., and the tithingman presenteth the boats of every tithinge, and all manner wreakes and deodannes happeninge within their several tithinges.

"*Other Customes and Orders approved by the Courts Rolles.*"

"It^m. That no ilander ought to marye his daughter oute of the island without licence of the lord constable or other officer.

"It^m. That no inhabitant of the ilande shall make any stone wall, hedge, or dyche above the assysse, that is no higher than that a hinde with her calf may easely leape over at all places.

"It^m. That no man ought to take or hunt any coneyes,

hare, ffox, or ffessaunt with dogges, nettes, or ferryatts within the warren, without licence or vewe of the warrener.

"It^m. That no man may enclose any of the wastes or heath within the ilande, without the vewe or licence of the warrener or the courte.

"It^m. That no sheriffe or bayliffe may arrest any tennaunts of the lord, or carry him out of the ilande, for any trespas.

"It^m. That no inheritor of the ilande may keepe, carry, or lead lose any dogges or curres in the heath or elsewhere, to the disturbance of the game, or to drive them out of their pastures.

"It^m. That no man within the islande may hunt any game from the first daye of Maye unto Holyroode Daye the last, upon payne of 6s. 8d,

"It^m. That no man ought to erecte or buyld upp any new howses in the heath or elsewhere without licence of the lord constable of the court.

"It^m. That no man's servaunt shall hunt within the warren but by the oversight of the waryners, upon payne of 2d. for every tyme.

"It^m. That no man ought to take any ffish on the Saboth Daye.

"It^m. That all ffishermen ought to keep their tydes, with their boats and ffishe, upon the sea costes by the custome.

"It^m. That all ilanders ought sufficiontly to fence their woods; and that they ought to keep out their cattayle out of their woods.

"It^m. That the keepers ought to apprehend and present all that harrie any of the nine coverts, or any other covert, and hedge tearers.

"It^m. Where by the word of the charter, viz., *(nullus piscator emens pisces)* it seemth that no ffishe takers be bounde to pitche their ffishe at the Corffe Cross: but the buyers only, and the ffishe takers to be at libertye to carry at their pleasure without that lett; yet it appeareth by the Court Rolles that as well the takers as the buyers have been amerced for that default from time to time.

"It^m. That the warreners and bayliffes may arrest bodyly for trespas against the lord of the castle, as well within Corffe as without.

"It^m. That the keepers ought to bring all such deare as they find dead or hurt to the Barbigan before the coroners."

A rather curious privilege was claimed on behalf of the King as lord of the warren of Corfe in favour of the two warreners and the ranger of the warren. By a custom called "methom," which it was alleged had existed time out of mind, the warrener and ranger were said to be entitled, after giving one day's previous notice, to be supplied by any tenant residing within the precinct and lordship of the castle, with board and drink, including three sorts of meat, one day in every week. But if such a day should be Tuesday or Saturday, or other vigil on which fish ought to be eaten, then fish of three sorts was to be set before them in lieu of meat. Food was at the same time to be supplied for their dogs.

In 23rd Ric. II. John Filoll, a resident tenant of the manor of Langton, within the lordship of the castle, having refused to supply the food demanded, his refusal was presented at the court of the warrener, held weekly by the constable at the castle gate, and his cattle were distrained. Denying the validity of the custom he brought an action against the warrener and ranger in the superior court in Michaelmas term, 4th Hen. IV., when the case was adjourned till the Hilary term following.* The result of the trial has not been met with.

* Plac. de Banco, 4th Hen. IV., m. 377.

APPENDIX.

(See page 64.)

It seems that this building must have been either a hall or a church, for it is pretty certain from what has been stated in the text that it could not have been a dwelling-house. The sloping floor would render it extremely inconvenient for a hall, even with such scanty furniture as might be found in an Anglo-Saxon residence, and its great length in proportion to the width would be but ill suited for a hall. Moreover, a hall must have formed part of a dwelling-house, whereas this building seems to have been detached and isolated. If an Anglo-Saxon mansion requiring a hall of these dimensions—and such a residence we may fairly assume would be in some degree made capable of defence—had adjoined this ruin, it would have been completely dominated by the hill immediately overhanging it. I think there can be little doubt, therefore, that whenever there was such a mansion at Corfe it was situated on the summit of the castle hill, and not on this spot, and it is not likely to have extended as far as to the platform below, for Anglo-Saxon houses were not very large.

Before laying open the foundations I rather expected to meet with traces of a chancel of narrower dimensions than the body of the building, which would have afforded unequivocal evidence that this was a church. None, however, were found; but such an arrangement was not necessary or always adopted in very early churches, some of which are built of uniform width, after the Roman manner.*

The nave and chancel of Deerhurst church, in Gloucestershire, which have herringbone work, and are supposed to have been erected before the Norman Conquest, are of equal width. They measure together fifty-nine feet in length by twenty feet six inches in breadth, and the chancel was originally still longer. The chancel of Morley St. Botolph, in Norfolk, is only three inches narrower in the inside than the nave, the whole measuring internally eighty-seven feet six inches by eighteen feet three inches.

The roof of the building at Corfe must have been of timber, as there is no indication of there having been any arches, or of any responds from which vaulting might have sprung. None such are mentioned by Bede and other ancient authorities in many churches which they describe.

The sloping floor of this building seems more indicative of a church than of a hall, for there are many examples of sloping floors in ancient churches in England.† The floor of the nave of Badingham church in Suffolk, is an inclined plane, rising about six feet in sixty, from west to east. The chancel, likewise, originally inclined, but less rapidly. The windows rise with the floor of the nave, as they do at Corfe. There was a church at Badingham when Domesday was compiled, and probably, therefore, it was built before the Conquest. The church now standing was most likely erected on the same spot as the original, and the sloping floor, therefore, may date from the Anglo-Saxon period. The floor of Berkeswell church, in Warwickshire, rises from the west end to the altar about three feet, and consists of several platforms with one or more steps between them. The second and third platforms are inclined planes, rising about one in twenty. The chancel is still more elevated. The floor of the church of St. Mary, at Guildford,

---

* The Basilica of Pompeii has a square end without an apse.
† See a notice of many of them in "The Antiquary," Vol. iii., p. 239.

in Surrey, is also an inclined plane, and has a very imposing appearance. Part of the church is said to date from before the Conquest.

These sloping floors of churches are in most cases accounted for by the slope of the ground on which they are built, and at Corfe it is evident that this part of the castle hill originally fell rapidly from east to west, though it has since been artificially formed so as to make two nearly level platforms, one of which is several feet below the other.

I am inclined to think that where the floor rose rapidly, on the site of the cross wall in the Corfe building, there must have originally been steps, as at Berkeswell.

The orientation of this building at Corfe, is as true as the ground will admit, being in the direction of E.S.E. by W.N.W., so that on the whole the evidence seems strongly to point to its having been a church.

Supposing that it was so, what was its age? I think there can be no doubt that a church was built in Purbeck by the Great St. Aldhelm, soon after the year 690, and William of Malmesbury says it was at Corfe. This seems to be the proper interpretation of a passage in his "Gesta Pontificum,"* supposed to have been written about 1105, not quite forty years after the Norman Conquest. He relates that Aldhelm being about to proceed to Rome,— whither he went between A.D. 690 and 700, to obtain privileges for his monastery,—visited his estates in Dorsetshire and built a church there, "*ecclesiam fecit*," two miles distant from the sea, and near Wareham, at the same place where Corfe Castle stands out in the ocean. "*Locus est in Dorsatensi pago ij milibus a mari disparatus juxta Werham ubi et Corfi Castellum pelago prominet.*"

Malmesbury adds that the remains of the church of which he was speaking still existed in his time, "*ejus domus maceriæ adhuc superstites*," but open to the heavens, being without

* Rolls series, p. 364.

a roof except something which overhung the altar, and protected the sacred stone from being defiled by birds. Notwithstanding its ruinous condition, whatever might be the violence of the storm which raged around it, not a drop of rain ever fell within the church, so that the shepherds of the district were in the habit of flying to it for shelter, regarding the phenomenon, not as a special miracle but as one of common occurrence. "Not to believe this" says the pious chronicler, "is great effrontery, since the declarations of so many who have had experience of it bear testimony to the fact." The nobles of the province, however, regarded it as a miracle, and several times endeavoured to restore the roof, but being unable to effect it had abandoned the attempt. They considered that it pleased the saint to adopt this means of manifesting his influence in heaven. Abundance of signs and miracles attracted people thither at the festival of the saint, and indeed the place was more famous for miracles than the abbey of Malmesbury itself, where St. Aldhelm's sacred bones were adored.

If we read Malmesbury's language literally, we can hardly avoid the conclusion that the church so described was at, or close to, Corfe, and at no great distance from Wareham. The expression, "*Pelago prominet*," seems to indicate that it was in the peninsula of Purbeck. If this was the case, the church could scarcely have been nearer to Wareham than at Corfe, for only a barren and uncultivated heath, nearly four miles in extent, lies between the two places, with the exception of Stoborough, which is so close to Wareham that a church could hardly have been required there.

It was an "ecclesia" and not an "ecclesiola" (a little church), the latter being the kind of Church which Malmesbury tells us St. Aldhelm built at Bradford-on-Avon. It, therefore, must have been intended for a considerable congregation.

There can be no doubt that Corfe must have been a "stronghold" from the earliest times, and as such it would be occupied by persons of power and influence. The population of the neighbourhood would naturally, therefore, congregate around a spot which afforded protection; and there is no other place in Purbeck, or elsewhere in the neighbourhood of Wareham, where a church is so likely to have been required as there.

The heath almost surrounds Wareham, extending northwards to a distance of between five and six miles. The town is seven miles from the nearest open sea, whilst Corfe is but a trifle over three in a direct line; and though neither of these measurements quite agrees with that given by Malmesbury, it can hardly be expected that a chronicler of the 12th century would be precisely accurate in estimating a distance of which he probably had no local knowledge, and which he had no reason to consider was of any moment. Corfe is a little over two miles from the Poole estuary, and Wareham is about a mile and a quarter; but the estuary would hardly have been designated *"pelagus."*

It is not necessary to suppose that because shepherds took refuge in this ancient building, it was situated in a remote and uninhabited region, where no other shelter could be met with, for Aldhelm would not have built a church where there was no population to frequent it. All the ground around the castle was most likely at that time open sheep walk, so that sheep must have fed up to the very walls of the building which then, no doubt, crowned the summit of the hill.

The foregoing facts seem sufficient to show that St. Aldhelm built a church in Purbeck, and that it was at Corfe. But whether it was identical with the herringbone building, part of which still remains standing, is quite another question.

There is nothing in the architecture of this fragment which is inconsistent with the theory that it is the remains of St. Aldhelm's church. Its very weather-beaten appearance, and peculiar method of construction, evidence its great antiquity; and its very small windows, though of less dimensions, are not unlike in character those of the "*ecclesiola*" at Bradford-on-Avon, which is still standing, and is admitted to have been built by St. Aldhelm, who has been described as "one of the greatest builders of his time."*

But there is no similarity between the masonry of the church at Bradford and the wall at Corfe. This, however, is easily accounted for. Masonry in all ages and in all countries has been influenced by local circumstances. Flint was generally used for facing walls in the eastern counties, and brick and wood intermixed were employed in Cheshire; but in Somersetshire and the adjacent part of Wiltshire, where admirable building stone, easily worked, was at hand, ashlar generally prevailed. At Bradford this facility led the builder of the "ecclesiola" to adopt the latter mode of construction, whilst in the remote district of Purbeck, though good building stone abounds, it lies deeply buried in the hills, and is for the most part very hard and difficult to work. It is possible, therefore, that in the 7th and 8th centuries few if any quarries might yet have been opened. But stone, thin and flat bedded, requiring no tooling, such as is used in herringbone work, is found near the surface, and is consequently easily acquired. The joints in Anglo-Saxon ashlar work were usually closer than in Norman buildings, and the worked stone of the windows of this building at Corfe is neatly tooled and closely fitted.

The preservation of the building—possibly in its integrity, but at all events its southern side when the more recent wall was built up against it—may not be without significance as indicating that some superior sanctity or importance was attached to it, arising, it is natural to suppose, from the miracles said to have been wrought there. Its retention could be of little use in strengthening the fortification, for the more recent wall outside it is 7 feet 6 inches thick, and is on the very brink of the castle hill, which is there too precipitous for a besieging force to find footing for attack, and, therefore, no

* Freeman,

extraordinary strength of wall was required at this spot. That the additional wall was of itself considered sufficiently strong is shown by its thickness not being increased after it quits the herringbone in its course towards the Butavant.

If, then, St. Aldhelm did build a church at Corfe, and if the very ancient building which has been described was really a church, is it unreasonable to conjecture that it may possibly have been the very same as that of which St. Aldhelm was the founder? The question is one which can never be conclusively answered; but whatever may have been the real date and destination of this building, its great antiquity admits of no doubt; and whether it is the remains of St. Aldhelm's church or not, I think it may be fairly assumed that Queen Elfrida herself either prayed or feasted within its walls.

There is a very small chapel, built probably in the 12th century, standing on the brink of the cliff on the extreme southern headland of Purbeck, and now known as "St. Aldhelm's chapel." It is square, and measures externally 32 feet; but this, or rather any earlier chapel, if any such stood on the same spot, could not have been the "ecclesia" mentioned by Malmesbury, for instead of being two miles from the sea, and near Wareham, it stands near the edge of the cliff; it is upwards of seven miles from that town and four miles from Corfe, in a direct line. Moreover, it is in so remote and wild a spot that it is difficult to conceive for what purpose an "ecclesia" (not an ecclesiola) could have been built there.

It has already been mentioned (p. 86) that in the Pipe Rolls of King Hen. III. and Ed. I. the chapel of St. Aldhelm, in Purbeck, and the chapel of St. Mary, in the tower of Corfe, are always mentioned conjointly. The salaries of the two chaplains ministering in both chapels are accounted for together, as if the services were performed by each in either chapel indiscriminately. If there was originally a church built by St. Aldhelm within the circuit of the present castle, the ruins of which still remained standing, it is likely that this fact may have suggested the idea of dedicating the more recent chapel to the saint whose name was still familiar in the neighbourhood as associated with the castle.

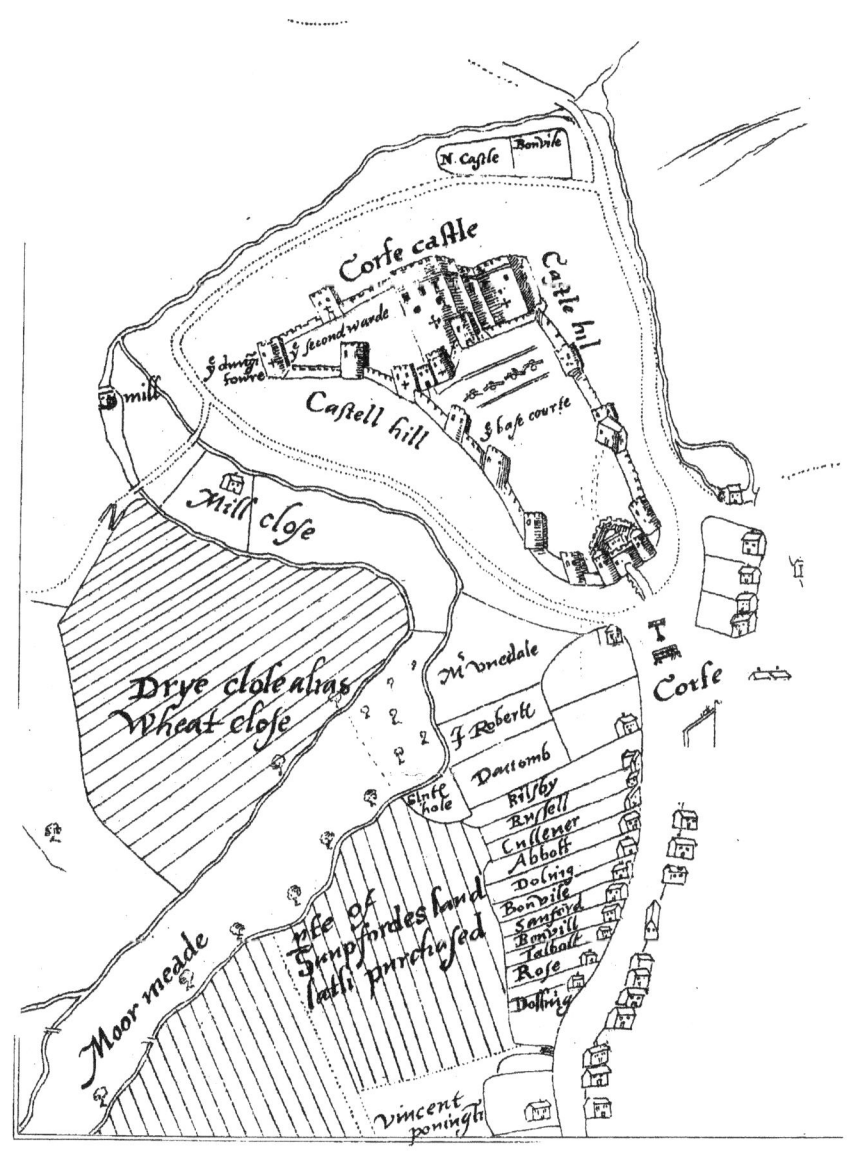

Fac-simile of birds-eye view of Corfe Castle, drawn by Ralph Treswell in 1586.

SEPTENTRIO.

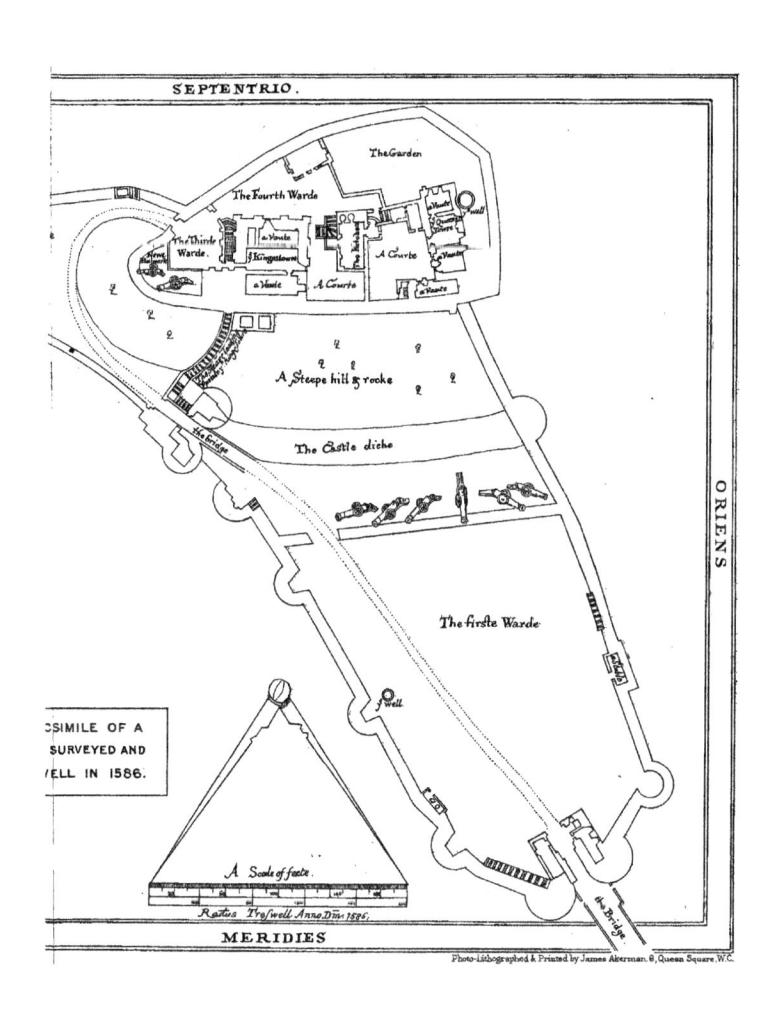

The Garden
The Fourth Warde
The Thirde Warde
a Vaute
Kingestown
a Vaute
A Courte
a Vaute
A Courte
a Vaute

A Steepe hill & rocke

The Bridge
The Castle diche

The firste Warde

ORIENS

a well

...SIMILE OF A
...SURVEYED AND
...ELL IN 1586.

A Scale of feete.
Robtus Treswell Anno Dm 1586.

the Bridge

MERIDIES

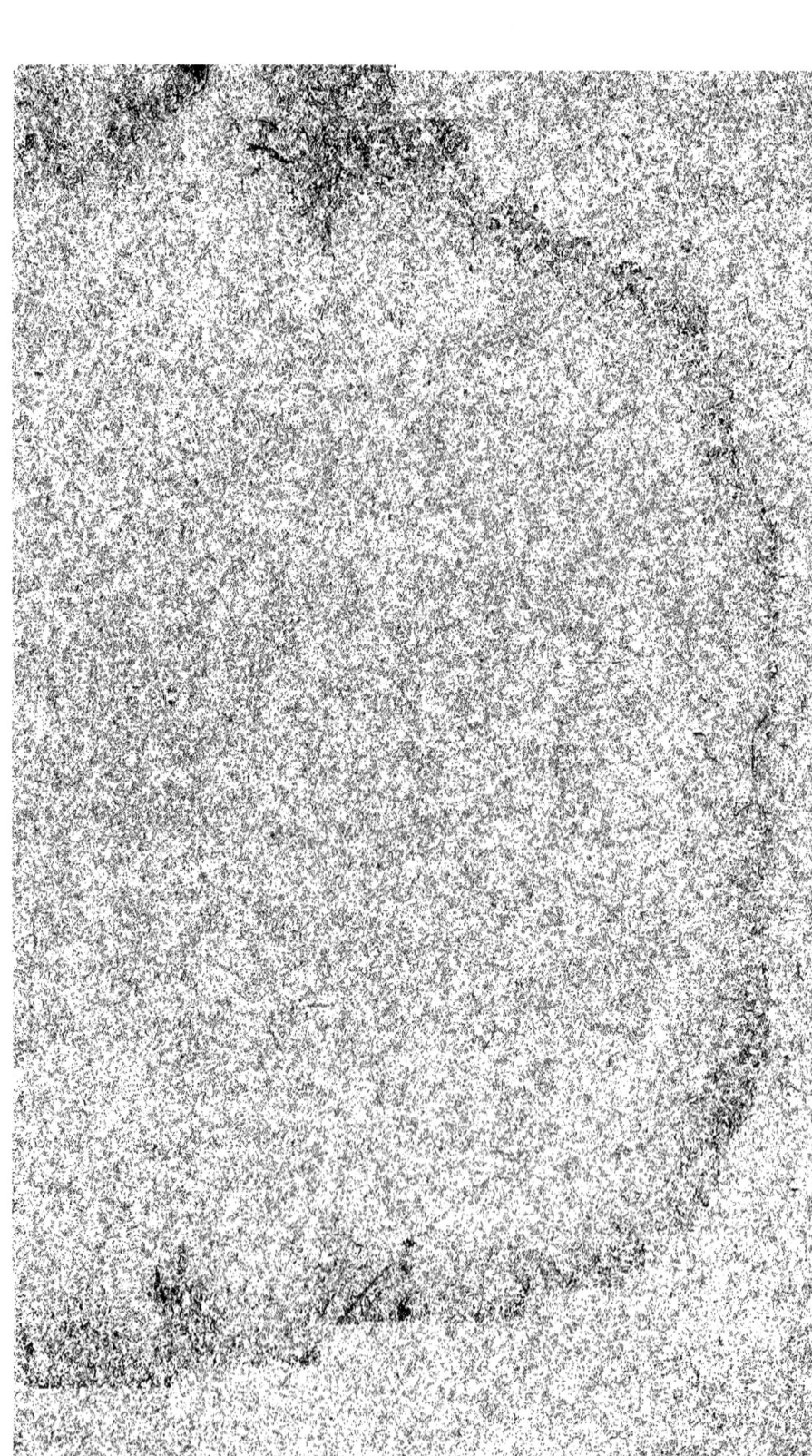

CORRECTIONS AND ADDITIONS.

Page 4, line 18, for "primœval" read "primeval."
,, 15, ,, 35, for "their" read "the"
,, 16, ,, 3, for "Arkenbeld" read "Arkenbald."
,, 23, ,, 11, for "hinself" read "himself."
,, 26, ,, 38, for "Lacay" read "Lacey."
,, 44, ,, 3 of note,* for "there" read "thence."
,, 48, ,, 25, and pages 95, line 29; 97, line 16; 98, line 18, for "foss" read "fosse."
,, 57, ,, 14, for "the" read "this" and omit "above it."
,, 76, ,, 5, for "slender shafts set in an angle," &c., read "A single slender shaft set in an angle on either side supports an impost."
,, 76, ,, 7, after "called" insert —
,, 86, ,, 24, for "2nd and 3rd" read 3rd and 4th."
,, 91, ,, 16, "The verdict thus shows that in the opinion of the jury on the evidence produced." &c. This is not literally accurate. The king in his writ broadly asserts, as if it was a well-established and well-known fact, that the castle of Corfe was "ancient demesne of the crown," and the jury, which was afterwards summoned to enquire respecting the liberties, rights and customs belonging to the castle, say nothing in their verdict to the contrary. The fact, therefore, seems to have been undisputed.
,, 114, ,, 33, for "vertiellos" read "vertinellos."
,, 115, ,, 6, for "Ed. I." read "Ed. III."
,, 130, ,, 11, "officials of the bishop"—Add foot note. "The Bishops themselves were usually fond of sport and they had a more dignified privilege than their officials, for when proceeding to hold their visitations at Corfe they were accustomed to hunt a doe in the chase of Purbeck. "*Unum cursum ad bissam habere consuevit.*"—*Inquis. 27 Ed. I. No.* 16.
,, 132, ,, 33, for "*subitus*" read "*subtus.*"

BOURNEMOUTH:
SYDENHAM & MACDONALD, PRINTERS.

SUPPLEMENTAL.

Page 80, line 26, "Chapel or oratory." Small chapels at the end of halls are described in the following terms by Mr. Freeman, in his recently-published "English Towns and Districts," page 37:—"St. Mary's Hospital, in Chichester, has a large hall opening at the east end into the chapel by an arch and screen. The object, of course, is to allow the inmates to attend divine service without going out of doors. The arrangement is the same as that which is found in many domestic castles and houses where the chapel was only large enough for the priest to say mass, while the household "assisted" in the hall or some other room from which they could look into the chapel. People who are not familiar with buildings of this kind are sure to mistake the hall for the nave of a chapel—the chapel, of course, being the chancel."

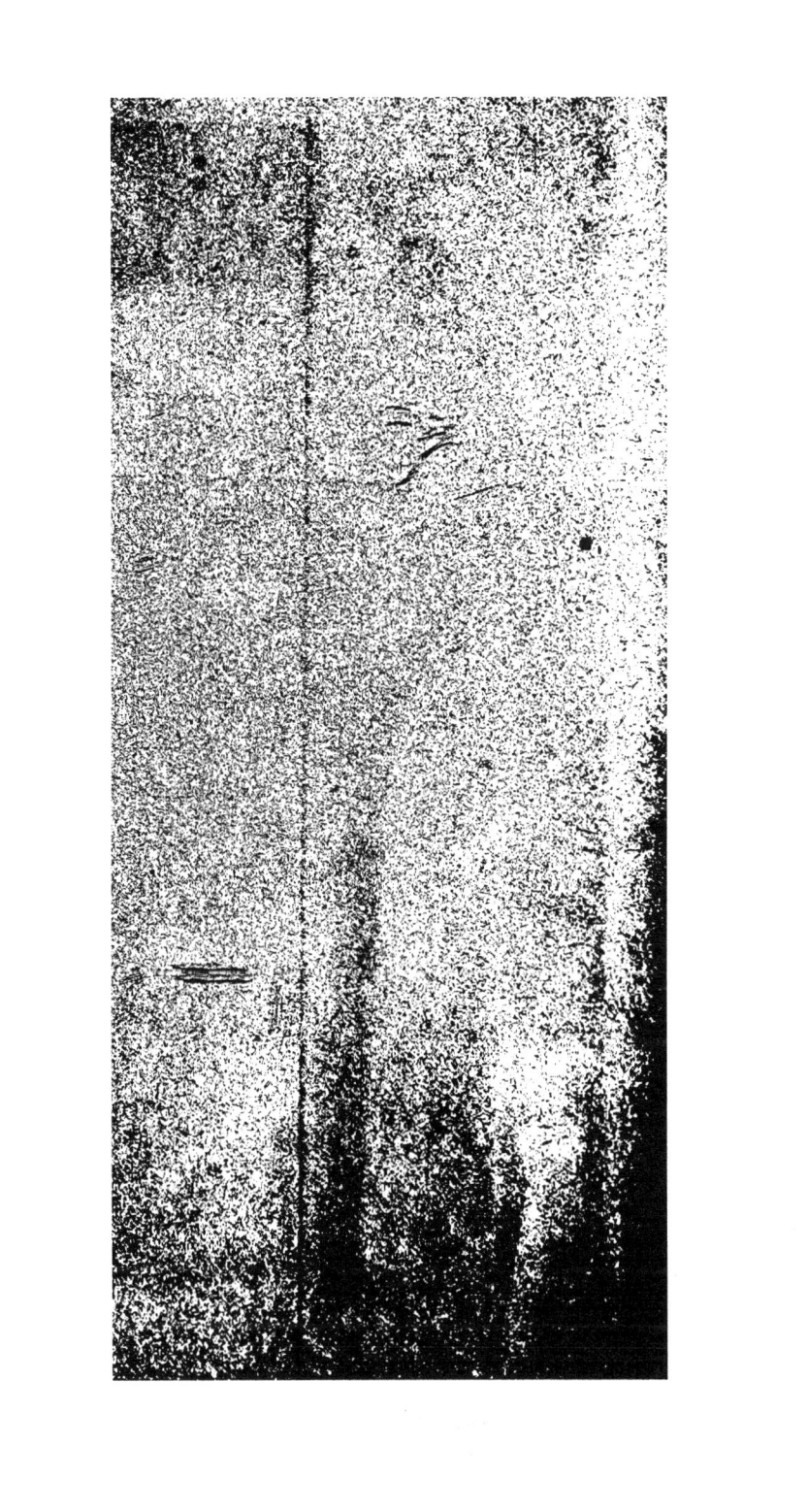

BOSTON PUBLIC LIBRARY

3 9999 06563 777 7

Boston Public Library
Central Library, Copley Square

Division of
Reference and Research Services

The Date Due Card in the pocket indicates the date on or before which this book should be returned to the Library.

Please do not remove cards from this pocket.

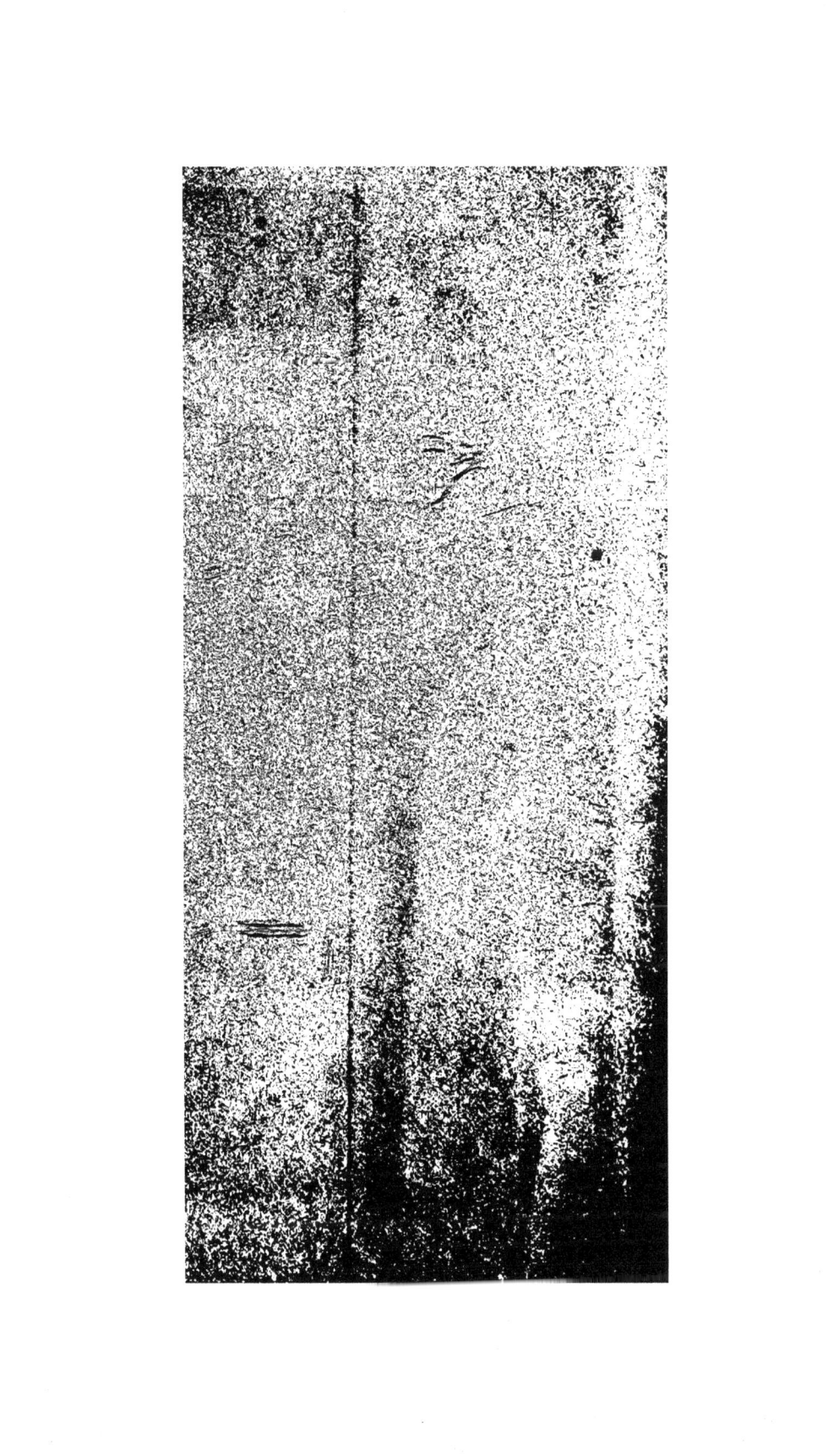

Boston Public Library
Central Library, Copley Square

Division of
Reference and Research Services

The Date Due Card in the pocket indicates the date on or before which this book should be returned to the Library.

Please do not remove cards from this pocket.